Praise for *Lost in Space*

"Ben Tanzer explodes the myths of fatherhood and reassembles the pieces into something altogether more precious and fascinating: the ugly, gorgeous, shameful, miraculous, transformative truth. This book is both funny and heartbreaking."**—Jillian Lauren,** *New York Times* bestselling author of *Some Girls: My Life in a Harem*

"In *Lost in Space*, Tanzer manages to be both heartbreaking and funny, producing a book of beauty and truth about the complexity, the fear, pain, and primal love that being a parent entails. Tanzer raises the bar with this memoir, insisting that writers be truly honest, not make excuses for their feelings, to stare deep inside themselves, and still be entertaining, if not enlightening."**—Paula Bomer,** author of *Nine Months* and *Baby*

"Ben Tanzer has that ever elusive elixir, that ability to be both funny and poignant simultaneously. These essays have that requisite gallows humor about being a parent, but there's tenderness oozing from the page, too, a kind of trickling empathy."**—Joshua Mohr,** author of *Fight Song*, *Termite Parade*, *Some Things That Meant the World to Me* and *Damascus*

"They said it couldn't be done. They said, "nobody dunks on Bill Cosby in the basketball court of dad-lit." And then Ben Tanzer's *Lost in Space* arrived. Funnier, more honest and a million times more relevant than the writing of JELL-O's favorite son, this tight little collection cuts to the soul of fathering children like nothing else."

—Patrick Wensink, author of *Broken Piano for President*

"Ben Tanzer's *Lost in Space* will have you vacillating between laughter and despair, all the while reveling in the beauty of his razor-sharp prose and candid, witty observations on fatherhood, sleep deprivation, Patrick Ewing, and family life. Buy this book, yo. And prepare to be astonished."

—Jennifer Banash, auth

Lost in Space

A Father's Journey There and Back Again

Space

Essays by
Ben Tanzer

Curbside Splendor Publishing

Published by Curbside Splendor Publishing, Inc., Chicago, Illinois in 2014.

First Edition
Copyright © 2014 by Ben Tanzer
Library of Congress Control Number: 2013957521

ISBN 978-0-9884804-6-9
Edited by Leah Tallon
Cover design and illustrations by Steve Lafler
Book design by Alban Fischer

Manufactured in the United States of America.

www.curbsidesplendor.com

For the boys, yo.

Contents

Lost in Space

I Need

I need sleep, long and deep and full of dreams about love, sex, pizza, Patrick Ewing, and *Caddyshack*. In these dreams I will be so happy, smart, funny, and full of *esprit de corps* that interns will float by my office in low-cut blouses begging to hear my innermost thoughts on *Game of Thrones*. I will not worry about bills or love handles, and I will not think about my children, not for even one moment, yo. If they happen to make an appearance they will say "excuse me," "yes," and "please," eat over the table using actual utensils, and not constantly bang their heads or mysteriously find their hands around the necks of one another.

Most importantly, they will go to bed when it's bedtime, after we've read together and nuzzled, and said our goodnights. They will just go to sleep, and if for some inexplicable reason they do not, they will still stay in bed. They won't wander around the house like extras from *The Walking Dead* in various states of duress, mumbling about how they cannot fall asleep, or how they heard something, and how I must have heard it too, "you heard it, right?" before asking me, "so could you just lie with

me for a little bit?" Nor will they come to my side of the bed during the middle of the night after I've already been asleep for hours, and loom over me, barely breathing, and ask, "I cannot sleep and what do you think about that?" I think I need sleep, motherfucker. Long and deep and full of dreams about Patrick Ewing, *Caddyshack*, and interns in low-cut blouses.

I also need to be able to control the weather. That's huge. My boys, well, my sons Myles, age eleven, and Noah, age eight, that is, not my testicles, don't like the wind. Rain is okay, if lacking in wind, and clearly identi-

fied by the Weather Channel as anything not related and/
or somehow connected to a monsoon, typhoon, tsunami,
cyclone, tornado, sharknado, hurricane, tropical storm,
or twister. Also, there cannot be any lightning, because
that will not fly. Snow is always fine, even a blizzard,
though not a blizzard that is especially windy, that's not
cool. Neither can said snow be mixed with lightning, so
no thundersnow sadly, or that weird thing when the
skies turn green.

I suppose what I really need to be able to do is control the wind. And what I really need to become is the
X-Men character Storm. You might know her as the su-
perhero portrayed by Halle Berry in the movies. And yes, I
need Halle Berry as well, though merely because she can
provide me with pointers. Wind means lack of control,
chaos, and instability, none of which the boys are totally
able to roll with. But when you live in Chicago, you can't
easily leave the house, or spend much time outside at
all. So, I really need these powers, and Halle Berry, and
if someone could give them to me, I can also see how
they would come in handy at those times when we are
flying and we get stuck on a tarmac for weather-related
reasons and are forced to consume all of the snacks, read
all of the books, play with all of the toys, and watch all
of the videos before we even take-off. Frankly, that sucks
and I definitely don't need that.

I do need to learn how to say, "Are you okay?" more
often. I learned this in family therapy. Apparently, when
a child of mine and I are in the midst of what is other-

wise a minor misunderstanding about what constitutes picking up one's toys, doing homework, taking a shower, brushing one's teeth, turning off the television, clearing the table, moving the laundry, talking respectfully, and using "I" phrases, and said child inadvertently trips over a toy or pile of laundry, slips in the bathroom, bumps into a closet door, bangs their head on a doorknob, cuts their finger, toe, elbow, knee, or ear, gets a headache, stomachache, or spontaneously combusts, my tendency is not to respond with, "Are you okay?" but something less empathic, and possibly in a voice not deemed sufficiently low, which I am told is not cool, and something I really need to do, which I will, promise.

Further, I need to be less fearful. I do not worry that my children will be kind and decent people at some still-to-be-determined point in their development, or that I can't be a father to boys as some of my friends have expressed to me because their fathers were not the role models they needed. But that's because these are rational fears, and I apparently can manage fears that fall into that category. It's the irrational fears that I need help with. And what are those fears? I'm glad you asked. In no particular order they are: childhood Leukemia; falling porches at crowded parties; stampedes in night clubs; gun violence, or any violence really, but especially gun violence; abductions: human, alien, or otherwise; plane crashes; drowning; broken necks; being run over by drunk drivers, or people texting, or any types of car accidents; plummeting from hotel or high-rise apartment decks; falling off of a cruise ship; sexual abuse, or any abuse frankly; brain damage; HIV/AIDS; drug overdoses; alcoholism; anorexia; bulimia; Obsessive-Compulsive Disorder; and cutting. All of which I need to chill the fuck out about. I know. But I can't.

Which might mean I need a vacation. Well, I do need a vacation, but let's be clear, that doesn't mean going to Michigan and renting a cottage with my wife and children, which I love doing, I do, or a hotel room in Madison or Milwaukee, Thanksgiving trips to Philadelphia, or Bar Mitzvahs on Long Island. It also doesn't mean going anywhere at all, if our children are with us, cool or otherwise, be that Thailand, Costa Rica, Peru, Spain, or Mexico. And this is not to say that I have deserted my dreams of hiking rim-to-rim across the Grand Canyon, walking out to Machu Picchu at sunrise, or triumphantly climbing Mt. Kilimanjaro with them, because I need to do all of that. Just as I need to see Barcelona, Rome, and Paris again, but with them, and through their eyes. But a vacation with them is not a vacation. I'm not at work, which is beautiful, and we're out of the apartment, which is also beautiful, but we're still together, which means children will be fighting, not sleeping, and there will be arguments. There will also be joy, a lot of it, but I will be on edge regardless, and what I need is for my wife Debbie and I to be somewhere where we are not putting children to bed, figuring out what children can eat, what they will find entertaining, or awaiting small bodies to loom over me at night like expectant vultures. I just need to sleep and run and read and Debbie sans children. I need it. Okay? Cool.

Finally, I also think I may need more patience, true patience, Zen, and serenity, so when one, or both, children says "I hate you" or "You suck;" or when they pee on the floor, spill drinks, don't check their homework, fight over who has to shower first, fail to use soap or shampoo; when they get out of bed, yet again, waking me from dreams about interns, *Caddyshack*, and Patrick Ewing; don't care that I am sick, had a bad day at work, got a bad book review, strained my back running, got into a fight with some asshole who cut the line at Jewel; I need to learn how to smile benevolently and think that this will pass. It is part of the journey, the journey is a long one, and the anger that has hold of me is useless, wasted energy, and then all of the bad feelings will dissipate as I find the needed grounding in my surroundings. I embrace that this is but one phase in the life I have created, and that regardless of what happens now or in five minutes, the Dalai Lama promised me during a dream last night, that when I am on my deathbed and I die, I will receive total consciousness, which is nice, because I need that too.

Towers

It has all the makings of a Hollywood love story.

We meet cute. We are in a hospital, and suddenly there is a blast of sunshine in an otherwise dreary, stressful world, rife with dead fathers, grandparents, and cousins.

You feel like you've known him his whole life, and from the start you can't help but think about your future together, the adventures you will go on, the conversations you will have, and the wonderfully unconditional nature of it all.

There will be bumps, of course, illness, issues with food and sleep. There will also be great frustrations and confusion, anger, and joy, but love as well, always, and tidal waves of it.

Maybe you're getting ahead of yourself here though, crafting the narrative you want and need. So you pause and just try to take it all in for a moment.

You are a father now, and it is a little heady.

That is all in the past now mind you, this is today, and today Myles is sitting there next to you on the plane, both of you crammed into coach, and its forced intimacy of dueling elbows, shared space, and endlessly touching knees.

His wool knit hat is long, floppy, black, and hip; the freckles on his nose are floating there, blurring across his beautiful skin; and his headphones are packed on tight, ensuring he won't miss a thing as he loses himself in *Mama Mia*, which is playing on the DVD player in his lap.

You don't want to stare, but that's impossible. You don't want to turn away though either, so you don't, not then anyway.

You suppose that at any moment he will turn to you and say, "What?" Or maybe he won't say anything. Instead he will just look and his expression will say it all, "What's your damage man?"

He doesn't turn though, too lost in whatever Amanda Seyfried is doing on the screen, and so instead the thought that comes to you, or maybe it's a feeling, is that you love him, that's all.

Mind you, even his birth wasn't exactly what you had been thinking about before this moment, before you got lost in his freckles, your love for him, and whatever else you've been swimming in.

You made yourself think about birth and love stories, because you had actually been thinking about another time, and another kind of intimacy, and you wanted to get a break from all that and think about happier things.

What you had been thinking about is how you were hugging him, tightly, and trying to breathe, calm down, and think peaceful thoughts.

But he was squirming, all bone, hot flesh, and anger.

The hug was intended to allow him to burn off some of the energy convulsing through his still small frame, though not as small as it once was certainly.

He is longer now, legs all akimbo, arms everywhere, like a newborn pony or maybe Mr. Fantastic on an especially bad day. He is not yet your height, but he will be sooner than later, each year inching closer, less like a weed than a tower, rising into the sky, fierce and proud, a reflection of your dreams and aspirations.

Of course, towers come down, we know that now, and is that too dramatic an analogy? Of course it is. And yet, this is about what you were feeling at that moment, anger, fear, weakness, futility, and love, endless and full of boundless emotion.

But let's come back to that as well, shall we? Because at that moment, you and he were in the middle of something and you didn't want anyone to get hurt, not him, especially, but not you either.

How did this start?

You don't know. It could have been anything, but let's call it sleep, because it starts there at times. Which you get, you do, you couldn't sleep when you were his age either, and your father could never sleep. It's a family curse. How's that for dramatic metaphors?

Still, he can probably relate to that. He loves fairy tales and princesses, and that which befalls them. Or he did anyway. He's older now, and he doesn't seem to do princesses anymore. It's all superheroes these days, but not all superheroes either, mind you. Not Thor, for example.

"Why not?" you ask him as you leave the theater, Noah all agog, Myles not so much. "What's wrong with Thor?"

"Seriously, he's a god." he says. "There's no back story there. Give me mutants and freaks and the characters who are like me please."

"Did you like anything about the movie?" you ask.

"I liked Natalie Portman," he says. "She's Jewish, right?"

It's about control, and for a kid who had colic, then hearing and speech problems, and is now trying to figure out how to fit in, control is important, needed, a lifeline, and his need for control can clash with your need for it. Something you're not sure you knew you even needed before he was born.

As you struggled with him, in that moment, the hug failing you, you thought, this is like a love affair isn't it? This is what it feels like—anger, joy, pain, frustration, longing, loss, excitement, sadness, confusion, desperation, desire—all of it, wrapped up in one moment, mashing together, twisted, and spent, but full of passion too.

From the start, your relationship with him prompted you to feel things you had not allowed yourself to feel before. Emotions you had hoped to bury or avoid. The idea of them embarrassed you. You were above all that, and not because you were better than anyone else, but because you were not willing to embrace any of it. It was all too messy and real.

But not with him, never with him, you can tell him you love him all day long.

You can also imagine shaking him, though. Something you never think about when dealing with adults. You know you're not supposed to feel this way, much less actually say it out loud, and it's not that you can truly imagine doing it, it's just that you can't not imagine doing it either.

He stops moving around so much.

"You can let go," he says.

Could you, though? Let go? Doubtful.

He was in a bad place that night, you got that. He felt out of control and he didn't know what to do with it, and you got that too. He told you that you can't possibly know what he's going through, and you don't think this is true.

Though that doesn't mean he isn't right.

There are many pieces of this that you don't understand. You didn't talk to your parents or storm around the house when things felt out of control.

You didn't do those things, so you can't really make sense of them. All of this may have to do with his feeling like an outsider, but you don't know for sure. What you do know is that he may be right about the fact that you don't know what he's going through, that you never really felt like an outsider.

Which would make him right, and that means admitting that you're wrong, not all-knowing, something people do when they're in love, make room for the possibility that they can learn from the other person, expose themselves to be flawed, and somehow seek to be empathic when everything the other person is going through seems so foreign and confusing.

"You can let go," he said more calmly and measured.

Could you?

You and Debbie had once been told that when he was feeling out of control you needed to hug him tight, pinning his arms underneath yours, and wrapping your legs around him until he burned off the excess energy and rage.

But no one had ever said how hard it would be or how long it would take.

"Why doesn't anyone talk about this shit," you asked an older colleague when he was still young and had colic.

"Because no one would have children," she replied.

But there you were, wondering when you should let him go, when's too soon, too much, and how do you ever really know?

And isn't that also what love is in all its awesome Air Supply cheesiness? Letting the other person be who they will be and loving them anyway, even when both of you may be enraged and confused, and the very act of loving them means you may have to let them go?

So, you asked yourself, could you let him go?

"Not yet," you finally say.

"It's cool," he says, "I'm cool. And I'm sorry."

You pause.

You feel him tense up.

"C'mon," he says.

"No," you say, "Not yet.

His body goes slack, he rests his head on your chest, and you stare at his sweaty brow.

"You don't love me," he says as towers crash everywhere.

The Champ

I was ten-years old when I went to see the movie *The Champ* with my friend Jim Collela. You may remember it. Jon Voight, now primarily known for wearing silk scarves to black tie events and fathering Angela Jolie, is a former boxer who works at the racetrack. His ex-wife is played by Faye Dunaway of *Chinatown* fame and that Bravo reality show about struggling actors. She is now remarried and loaded. His son is played by the incredibly cute Rick Shroeder, who was still known as Ricky then, and way more *Silver Spoons* than *NYPD Blue*.

Ricky has christened Jon "Champ" and wants him to start boxing again. After Champ finally acquiesces, they run along the beach together, there are some horse racing scenes, and then Champ fights. He might even win, but he's old, and Champ receives an incredible Tex Cobb-style beating. When they lay him down on the trainer's table after the fight he's clearly dying and Ricky starts hitting him on the chest with his little fists, sobbing, and screaming "Champ" over and over again. But it doesn't help. The motherfucking Champ dies, just like that, even as young Ricky tries to will him back to life.

The scene borders on emotional torture, possibly even death porn. *Old Yeller* crossed with *Beaches*—with a touch of *Terms of Endearment* and *The Lion King* thrown in for laughs. As I watched it I wanted to cry as well. I was dying to cry, but I wouldn't let myself do so. In part I would have never let myself cry in front of Jim, but the problem wasn't just my unwillingness to risk future playground mockery by crying in front of a friend. I would never have let myself cry then regardless of the circumstances.

I didn't cry when I was ten because tough guys didn't cry. And how did I know that? Because my father who valued toughness as much as anything, never cried at all, ever, done.

Myles, Noah, and I are watching *Up*. They have seen *Up* already with my mom, but Debbie is out of town, it's a boys' weekend, and they want to do something special. They want the three of us to go to a movie theater and see *Up* together.

Ellie, the wife of Carl, the old man protagonist in the movie, dies almost immediately because that's what they do in kids' movies: kill moms, or wives, sometimes dads, and while this usually doesn't affect me very much at all, Ellie dying absolutely destroys me.

I think this is partly because of what Ellie had been, this terribly adventurous kid with these terribly big plans to explore the world, versus what she had become, an old woman who hadn't done any of that. Ultimately, she found herself happy, but trapped, wanting something more, but forced to settle for less.

Then she goes and dies, happy, but still trapped, and that's too much for me to bear.

This theme is always bound to kill me, because I inevitably think about my father. He was an artist who never felt he got his due and endlessly felt trapped by his inability to figure this out. The decisions he made, and did not make, including, leaving New York City and Washington, D.C., moving to the small town I grew-up in, parenting, and on and on.

"Are you crying?" Myles says, partly astonished and partly full of glee.

"You shouldn't talk during the movie," I say, quickly, so I don't have to answer him, or tell him I'm not crying, because reflexively that's what I do, or want to do anyway.

I am not embarrassed, though, really. Still, I don't respond.

"You are," he says. "Awesome."

My father Michael Tanzer was not just a painter, he was also a tough guy from the Bronx who was nicknamed "The Rock" long before the other, slightly larger Rock was ever born, and he never quite achieved the kind of success as an artist he longed for.

For much of my life I could only recall having seen him cry once. We were at his father's funeral, which was at this ancient Jewish cemetery in Queens. It was a blustery day straight out of movie-making 101, with the wind, the bleak skies streaked with rain. My dad was standing next to his two younger brothers. One after the other, they read passages from the Torah. I had never heard Hebrew before, and I had no idea that my father could read it, but when it was his turn, his face became contorted in a way that I had never seen before. It was suddenly all lopsided and sinking and as he slowly transformed into this incredibly sad gargoyle, the tears grudgingly came.

It was the worst thing I could ever imagine having to watch, but then my dad was the worst crier I have ever met. Later, when he was dying and began crying with some frequency, it always looked like such an effort for him that it barely mattered to me what he was crying about because I always felt bad that he was struggling so much.

He wasn't comfortable being around tears, and not necessarily because tears were a sign of weakness, though this was what I assumed when I was a child, but because they were so raw, and so painful, and I'm not sure he could bear to be around that kind of pain.

Which leaves me where?

I am a father, who is the son of a tough guy who never cried, I never cried as a child, and now I have two children, sons no less, sorry, who cry all the time.

What is the normal amount of crying though, and what is acceptable in terms of what they cry about? For example, here is a short list of what tends to make them cry—doing homework; the rules around watching television, how often, how long, and what; my mom leaving; my mom dying, someday; death in general;

banging their heads, arms, legs, toes, ears, or backs, on anything, any time, which may be legitimate; eating vegetables; *LOST*; fatigue; wind; dogs; bedtime; hunger; showers; and socks, including, but not limited to the socks' inability to fit right, line-up correctly, and generally not bunch-up around the toes, heels, the top of the foot, or sole.

It's not that I want the boys to think that crying is a sign of weakness like I do. Nor do I want them to think that you aren't tough if you cry. However, I am my father's son, and I'm not sure I truly feel that way despite how often and easily I now cry myself.

Which is not to say that I don't get it, or that I haven't gotten it sooner than my father did, it being the idea, that it's an awesome thing to be in touch with pain, it's just that I'm not sure I quite trust the feeling, I can only re-learn so much.

I suppose this means, that I am a self-hating crier.

I suppose this also means that I owe you a short list of what makes me cry as well. And that's no problem, really—*UP*, clearly; *The Lion King*; the play *Blood Brothers*; the occasional reality show, including but not limited to any participants with any kinds of challenges, be they mental, physical, violence, or substance-abuse related; *Friday Night Lights*, the book, movie, or television show, though especially the latter; the scene in *Mississippi Burning* when the father is hung by the KKK and the son finds him, or any scene any time when a father dies, see *The Lion King* above; watching the boys perform on stage, get haircuts, or run; almost anything involving them frankly.

But not socks. Socks don't ever make me cry. Nor do physical injuries, not often anyway.

When I was nineteen I spent the summer mowing lawns and I caught my hand in the blades of a lawn-mower. I would like to tell you that it was a freak acci-dent, but that's not quite the truth. It's true that the lawn-mower didn't work exactly. You had to muffle the engine to turn it off. It's also true that on that day I was muffling the engine. But while I'm kind of certain that the engine turned off and then on again, a risk you ran if you didn't fully muffle it, I can't truly say for sure.

Things got real quiet after that though, there was lots of blood and I found myself supporting my mangled hand on an old McDonald's bag as I was rushed to the hospital.

I got to the hospital just after the victims of a big car accident had been brought in, and the accident victims were so fucked-up, and needed so much attention, that there was no one left to take care of me. The nurses in-sisted I would be fine, and with no available doctors there wasn't much they could do regardless. They left me off in a room of my own, with people screaming all around me, and my hand slowly starting to stiffen.

I began to panic. I was in shock. I was alone. And there were those screams. But then the curtains parted and there was my dad, decked out in his usual uniform of ratty jeans and an old Oxford shirt of mine. He looked at me, and this terrible sadness suddenly permeated the room. Neither of us said anything.

I started to bawl. I hadn't cried for ten years, but I was ready to let it all out, all the tears I had skipped, all the emotions I had suppressed.

My pops just kind of stood there for a minute.

"You don't need to cry," he finally said.

"I really do," I said looking right at him.

With that he walked over grasped my good hand and let me cry. Neither of us said another word until my mom arrived.

After that I began to cry a lot, but I still never saw my dad cry, not until he got sick.

About a month before my dad passed away, a Lubavitcher rabbi he had befriended offered to come to the hospital and do a Yom Kippur service for him. The rabbi, decked out in a black coat and suit, a black fedora pulled down tightly around his head, his paes' curling into his fantastically full beard, arrived with his young daughters, and a young follower, who had come to blow the Shofur, or ram's horn.

He performed the service and the little girls sang, and as we sat there transfixed, my father's eyes began to brim with tears. The young follower then blew the Shofur seven times, and each time he did the intensity of my father's crying grew stronger. I was now accustomed to him crying, but I had never seen him cry quite like this.

"Mike, what are you feeling," my mom asked after the ceremony was over.

There is some debate between my mother and me

about his answer. My mother believes he told us that with each note of the Shofur he felt he was being healed. I believe he told us that with each note he felt more at peace. And our memories may be less reflective of what he actually said, and more reflective of how we need to remember the event.

Either way, we were both left with the same thought, what if he had cried more during his life? Would he have been at greater peace with himself? Would he have known himself better? Would he have felt less trapped?

We cannot answer those questions, but I can ask myself whether those same questions apply to me, or the boys, who are both so open to crying at ages that I was not; and I can wonder whether they will be better versions of me and my father.

I would like that, assuming of course they stop crying over putting on socks or taking showers, because crying at those times just isn't tough, and while I hate myself for even thinking it, I have to draw the line somewhere.

Bed Sex

We are hosting a dinner party, we've ordered-in from Old Jerusalem on Wells, people are over, the boys are running around, and someone swears, possibly me, not that I would ever curse in front of my children, that is wrong.

Everyone stops speaking, however, and said curser looks at the then nine-year Myles sheepishly, who in turn responds, "It's okay, I've learned all the bad words at school."

Wonderful.

"You did?" I say.

"Yeah," he says proudly, "like the 'd' word is dumb."

Everyone laughs.

"The 's' word," he says, "stupid."

More laughs, and some relief.

"And the 'b s' word," he continues, "bed sex."

Everyone smirks. It's cute, sort of.

"Bed sex," I say, "who told you that one?"

When I say this, I try not to sound too dad. I want to sound cool. Which I could tell you is generally not so important to me. But that would be BS. And not the bed sex kind.

"Melissa," he says, "she watched the movie *Australia* while her grandmother was sleeping on the couch, and she told us everything."

What?

"And she was talking about how the girl has to be on top of the boy," Myles continues, "for it to count. And that's bed sex."

Melissa, of course, this is a re-occurring theme of hers.

She also told Myles how her parents schedule their days off at the same time so they can stay home and have sex while she is at school.

Bed sex presumably?

Later that night, as she is wont to do, Debbie says, "You need to talk to him, soon, now even. And don't say you will in the same way you say you'll clean the bathtub and then don't for weeks."

"Why me?" I say feebly. "No one ever spoke to me about sex."

"Exactly," she says, "and look at the years of confusion and suffering that have resulted for both you and the women in your life. It's not right."

She's right of course.

But, is it true that no one in a position of authority ever spoke to me about sex?

It is.

Not a sentence. Nor tip. No warnings. And nothing about mechanics.

Is it also true that when I was twelve I read about a

book titled *Boys and Sex* and then asked my father to drive me to a bookstore so I could buy a copy of said book?

It is.

The cover was blue, of course, and the topics covered included among other things pubic hair, masturbation, and homosexuality, all of which I had a passing knowledge of, which is to say almost none.

You might wonder if my father thought he should ask me some questions about the book, what I had read, or thought, did I have any questions for him. And he might have thought about that, but if you were to wonder if he actually asked me any of those questions, the answer is no, not at all, never, not once.

Which also means, that I never quite had any idea what I was going to do if, and when, sex became a possibility for me.

Not long after I read, and re-read, *Boys and Sex*, I read and re-read, *The Chocolate War* by Robert Cormier until the paper cover was tattered and small pieces of the spine crumbled into my hands every time I read it. It was the story of a private, Catholic high school, class structure, norms, and Jerry, a freshman football player who cannot fit in, and will not fit in, but receives an assignment from the Vigils, the secret society at school, to fuck with the annual chocolate sales, by refusing to sell chocolate for 10 days. Jerry embraces the challenge however, long beyond the ten days as the ultimate fuck-you to the school and its strictures.

I was captivated by the book as a whole and its message of whether any of us dare "disturb the universe," but what I was especially fixated on was Jerry's fear that he might never touch a girl's bare breasts. It was as painful and confusing to me as anything I had read in the book and it spoke to my belief, that everything made sense to everyone but me, including how one touched a bare breast, or possibly even two.

The Chocolate War also served as a contrast to my favorite book then and now, *The Basketball Diaries* by Jim Carroll. Jim Carroll got over and Jim Carroll seemed just barely older than me, and yet he seemed to know, and do, everything.

Whereas, I, like Jerry, knew nothing, and did nothing, and it wasn't clear to me how any of that was going to change.

It didn't, not immediately, and yet there I am one night just a couple of years later drinking with one of my friends, and there is a moment when she looks at me in a way she never has before.

"Should we go upstairs?" I ask, trying to sound confident as I assume that this is the kind of moment that John Hughes keeps writing about, the opportunity to be with someone I may never have the chance to be with again.

Soon we are looking for an open bedroom and being upstate New York in January when we do find one, the bed is covered with winter coats, puffy and soft, and sort of perfect really for what I hope is about to go down.

As we start to kiss, I begin to wonder how one gets to second base. Do you ask? Do you go for it? And how soon do you do either? I cannot figure any of this out, so I reach down to lift up her navy, rag wool, L.L. Bean sweater.

She says nothing.

I continue.

I quickly encounter a button down Oxford, a collared Polo shirt, a J. Crew T-shirt, and finally a long-sleeve thermal shirt so tightly adhered to her skin that I have to pry it off. There is no hesitation on her part, and so I continue, only to encounter her bra, which has a front snap. What is that? I've never seen one of those in a movie.

And yet it unhooks, and there are two breasts before me, and like Roger Bannister, I cross a barrier previously considered unattainable for otherwise mortal men.

This mortal man anyway.

My friend and I hook-up again sometime after that, and for a brief, terrifying moment I even think she will be the first person I sleep with. But there's too much alcohol involved, and none of the magic that accompanied our previous encounter.

When we are adults we will talk about those nights, and as she looks down at her not quite bodacious chest, she will tell me that she feels bad for being my first.

I don't feel that way though, I still feel grateful. I also feel like I still have no idea what I'm doing, and that never changes.

So, whether I am equipped to have sex, much less discuss it, or offer advice about it, is questionable, very questionable, but not optional as the father of a nine-year old boy who is friends with girls who apparently are wildly misinformed on the topic.

The next day, before dinner I pull him aside.

"Dude," I say, trying not to be weird or too nonchalant, "we need to talk after dinner."

"Can we wait until after dessert?" Myles says.

It is here when I am reminded that I am talking to a little boy. He may think he knows something about sex. He may also think it's important to assert this. But nothing is more important than dessert, or more importantly that he might miss it because I have something I want to talk about.

After dessert, he leans against his bed as cool as a cucumber, and I do the same against his brother's bed, though not quite as cool, and given my advanced age, much less cucumber-like.

"We need to talk about sex," I say.

"I knew it," he says, jabbing his finger at me. "I knew this would be the sex talk."

My goal here is to be scientific, just the facts as best as I can provide them. I will be sparse, I will stick to the basics, I will focus on mechanics, and I will try not to smirk.

"Okay," I start, "do you understand how people get pregnant?"

"Yeah," he says, "the boy puts his penis in the girl's mouth."

Yeah, maybe on a really good day I think, or like an anniversary or something.

"Yeah," I actually say.

"Yeah, and then the sperm goes down to their stomach, and the girl gets pregnant, right?" he says.

Wow, no, not at all, how can he think that?

I try to remember how I thought someone got pregnant when I was his age, but I'm not sure I thought about it at all beyond studying a *Penthouse* magazine we had in an attempt to better visualize how people fit together.

"Not exactly," I actually say, "the boy has to put his penis in the girl's vagina."

"What, ew, no way. Really?" he says looking at me incredulously, and not as cool as a moment earlier.

"Yes," I say as professorially as possible, "and then the sperm finds, or swims, its way to the girl's eggs, and if all goes right, the sperm fertilizes the egg and conception has occurred."

"So that's bed sex?" he says.

"That's sex," I say, "or intercourse."

"Bed sex?" he says again.

"You know, sweetie," I say, "all sex is bed sex, because most of the time you are in a bed, not always, but most of the time."

For a moment I lose myself in the fact that I once wondered if I would ever touch a woman's breasts and now I not only get to have sex, but I have to talk about it.

"So you're not always in a bed?" he says waking me from my reverie.

Shit, I needed to stop sooner than that, yo.

Again, I have to ask myself, whether I am trying to be too cool? Probably, and I need to ratchet it back.

"I don't think we need to cover that today," I say, "but do you have any more questions about conception?"

"Can you have sex standing up," he says, ignoring me.

It sort of depends on the angle, and height, I don't say, trying not to think about *Less Than Zero* and Robert Downey Jr. banging Jamie Gertz in that alley.

"Or in a garbage can?" he continues.

Only after a number of drinks, maybe, not likely, but sure, why not? Not that I say this either.

"The important thing," I say both wanting to move him off of this thread and not be all about science when sex is so much more complicated and better than that, "is that people don't only have sex so they can have babies. It's fun too, and pleasurable, and it is very hard to put off having sex once you want to have it, but if you can wait until you're older and more mature, it will be better, I promise."

To this he says nothing, and while there are a million other things I want to say, it's not the time.

This is a victory though, I did something I arguably didn't want to do, that no one did for me, and I got through it, if not with flying colors, with something anyway.

"Hey," I say to him while patting myself on the back, "do you have any more questions?"

"No," he says, "that's enough for now."

I Believe in You (Sketches on the Younger Child)

1.

Charlie, the junkie one-time rock star on *LOST*, is a younger brother. In the beginning he is a serious musician, and a good boy, proper, and studious. But that is before he follows his older druggie brother and charismatic lead singer of their band down the road of groupies, addiction, excess, and rot. This shouldn't surprise us, however. Younger brothers idolize older ones. Older brothers are both substitute parent and friend. They have the wisdom that comes with having lived longer, and they are happy to impart it, right or wrong, to their most loyal audience. Charlie ultimately cleans up, falls in love, does good, and finds redemption. But he still dies on a God forsaken island off in some magnetic geographical zone that maps cannot track, much less locate. I am hoping for better with Noah.

2.

There is a homeless woman who works the door at the Jewel in our neighborhood. She sells *Street Wise*. She's not pushy or loud, and yet I find her off-putting. It might be the stringy hair or parched skin, but I don't think it's her appearance. Well, I hope not. What I believe, is that she oozes desperation in such a passive manner, blending in, but always there, staring, waiting, wanting, that it angers me. The other regulars in the neighborhood are smoother, engaging, making conversation, and asking about the boys, but not her, not ever. She just stands there, and even just writing this reminds me how self-conscious I am about my reaction to her.

Despite this, I do not give her change, though I regularly give change to other homeless people, both men and women, in the neighborhood, and down by my office.

While I always feel bad about this, I feel much worse about it when I am with the boys, and especially when I am with Noah, who doesn't talk much yet.

I don't know what goes on inside Noah's head. He's not like Myles who is so external, expressing everything, every feeling, thought, and question.

He's the younger brother, and there isn't much air space for him. But he's watching, and he is sponging-up everything around him all the time. He's just doing it as younger siblings do, silently and stealthily, moving along, watching, and gathering information about whatever he's trying to make sense of.

One day Noah and I are in Dunkin' Donuts and the homeless lady is standing there, not talking, just waiting, waiting for something, and in my head, passing judgment on me, my lifestyle, and my unwillingness to share any of that with her.

Noah is intently watching her, and I am watching him, cognizant of his presence, and of wanting to be better than I normally am for reasons both selfless and self-serving.

I ask her if I can buy her a cup of coffee and a donut. She says yes, and Noah doesn't say a word, instead slowly, and quietly, consuming his Vanilla Long John, small bite by small bite.

Months later as we are walking home from school, we pass the woman on the street in her usual spot by the Jewel, and Noah, who has otherwise been silent, speaks.

"People don't like to give her money," he says, at once both matter-of-factly and quizzically.

"You're right," I say, "why do you think that is?"

"I don't know," he says, "but you bought her a cup of coffee and a donut and that makes you a good person."

"I hope so," I say.

3.

Prince Harry is also a younger brother. He is prone to dressing like a Nazi for costume parties and racing Olympic Gold medalist swimmers in the buff. He also looks a lot like his dead mother's former bodyguard, and very little like his brother or father. He still has to compete with his older brother's awesomeness, however, and how much Prince William looks, and acts, like their mother, the most beloved woman in the world at the time of her death. That can't be easy for Harry, and I'm glad Noah doesn't have to worry about any of that. Debbie has never had a bodyguard.

4.

When Myles was five years old he had a thing for the Disney princesses—the movies, their ice shows, and the ways they might interact with the Power Rangers if just given the chance. He also had a thing for princess figurines, which he liked to place strategically around the house.

When Noah was 17 months old, he followed Myles around, wanting to do the things Myles did, and wanting to like the things Myles liked. Which in those days were those princess figurines. I don't think Noah cared about their back story, or how they looked on the ice. Myles loved them, and so would he.

At first this was cute. Noah would walk around and gather as many of them as he could, and then as he had seen Myles do he would arrange them in the different locations that he could reach. He would work his way around the house, focused, diligent, and going about his business.

Then something changed.

First, Noah grew upset if he couldn't pick-up all of the figurines at once. And then he started to get upset if he didn't have at least one in each hand at all times. He soon had to have some in his crib when he went to bed and he always woke-up scrambling to figure out where they had gone during the night.

An action that had started off as modeling and idealization had morphed into something he needed so he could feel ownership over a world that didn't always make sense, a world where everyone he knew regularly came and went to school and work.

It's not like we didn't know this was coming, we read *Peanuts*, and when Myles was Noah's age he latched onto a teddy bear, which though long washed-out and faded, he still calls Rainbow Bear and sleeps with to this day.

What we didn't know is whether this was a phase that would evolve in a healthy fashion as Noah continued learning how to self-soothe.

Like with Myles and his bear, Noah was still a little ball of clay being shaped all the time, and while I wouldn't want to know Noah's future if I could, I also know I wouldn't have to worry so much if I did.

Noah outgrew those figurines, but like Myles he became frightened by dogs and the wind, things we have no control over as we try to make our way through the world.

Myles is no longer afraid of dogs. It's how he is. He decided he was done with that, and that was that. We are still waiting for Noah to get there.

5.

Casey Affleck has benefited from his older brother's benevolence, see *Gone, Baby Gone*, and by trying to be nothing like him. He makes small movies. His relationships are private. And he seems to be surrounded by as little drama as possible. Younger brothers have to go their own way even when they are on the same path as their older brothers, but it's certainly easier to do so, when how to do so is clear and your older brother is there to guide you.

I hope Myles knows this, or if he doesn't, that he learns it, because Noah will have many challenges, and while he will make many mistakes, I don't see any reason for both of them to make and repeat the same mistakes again and again.

6.

Some things about Noah that you don't know:

He likes to stroke Debbie's hair while watching television or going to sleep, but he will stroke mine or his own as needed.

When he first started speaking he couldn't say the word "disgusting," and it always came out "puh-scusting." He also had a problem pronouncing "hallelujah."

For a long time, he had only one adult tooth come in, and it was enormous and weird, and awesome to behold when he laughed

By the end of the day, now that he is talking a lot, Noah's voice grows very raspy, like Brenda Vaccaro's. It always seemed very cute, but may eventually require surgery.

Noah cries when he cannot make his socks fit, which is often, and one of the many reasons I love the summer. He wears sandals every day.

He calls soccer practice "soccer class," and like regular class, he talks about Pokemon the whole time he is there with his friend Harper.

When Noah smiles, he sometimes looks like my grandmother, though at other times he looks like my father-in-law. It's all about how much he scrunches his eyes and opens his mouth.

He doesn't like jokes about death because he thinks that when people make them around me I will get sad about my father having passed away.

7.

Sometimes younger brothers take care of older ones. Theo Van Gogh apparently did the best he could to ensure that Vincent was stable, productive, and able to sell his work. Vincent's story didn't turn out so well, but it seems like it could have been worse, which offers me some solace as the father of two boys.

8.

They say younger siblings grow-up in different families. That they get less attention and fewer photos. That they have to be tougher, and cuter, and that they are endlessly compared to their older siblings, for reasons both good and bad.

They also have the benefit, though, of having parents who have done most everything before, are less stressed about safety and the inclination to hover, and are generally too tired to care about the things that somehow seemed so important the first time around.

And of course you can't care about everything, because having more children is not just two or three times as much work, it's something more inexplicable than that. What is quite explicable, however, is that anything remotely resembling down time has vanished.

They have the same needs, however, the newer ones, but sometimes you are just holding on. You are calmer, yes, but exhausted too, and just want the crying, fighting, moaning, whining, sniffling, complaining, yelling, and general loudness and overwhelming sense of being on, forever on, to just dissipate, if not outright go away for a moment, or more.

Though even a moment is a blessing and happily embraced.

And so there is Noah, the younger one, so yummy from jump that I could just eat him, and I would, all of him, gulping him in massive bites, and not stopping to catch my breath for even a second. He's like a donut, a grimy, oozy, sticky, crying powdered donut that I just want to touch and smell and curl-up with at every moment possible.

Despite this, do I automatically accept that he must still somehow get less attention than Myles, did, and does, based on the fact that he is the younger one? Yes, probably. There was one, and now there are two, and there is less to give.

Which is a cop-out for sure, but not nothing either.

I am present though aren't I? I am, and I am engaged, yes? Yes, though am I less engaged than I was with Myles before Noah came, maybe but how should I measure that? I can't, or won't, and yet there we are at the kitchen table one day, doing his fractions homework.

Noah is hunkered down, pencil in hand, eyes focused,

brow furrowed. His beautiful, buttery skin is so ripe I just want to eat him on the spot.

I try not to stare, but it's impossible.

"I'm not sure I can do it," he says suddenly looking-up at me with his endlessly brown eyes. "You can," I say, "I believe in you."

"You've never said that to me in my entire life," he says, smiling and getting back to work.

Who knows, maybe I haven't said that before to him. He is the younger one, and things get overlooked. I will say it from now on though, always, or as long as he lets me anyway.

9.

My mother once told me that your sibling is the friend you will have the longest. I never questioned this, I just didn't think about it. And yet, here we are, my younger brother Adam and I, forty years on, drinking and running and talking about *WTF with Marc Maron*, marriage, parenting, and Presidential elections. Adam still asks for my advice on things, which I find amazing and humbling. I take the role of older brother very seriously and I always have. I hope Noah and Myles have that. I also hope I get to see it, because the idea of it sounds wonderful to me.

The Mel Gibson Interlude: Or, What We Talk About When We Talk About Movies

When Myles was younger, and long before there was a Noah, my therapist told me about the great pleasure he derived from watching *The Godfather* with his son when he turned 16 years of age. I started calculating then what Myles and I, and now Noah, would some-day watch together, and though these plans have been fraught with challenges—for example, after watching *High School Musical* for approximately the fiftieth time, I stated that I couldn't wait until Myles was old enough to watch the movies I wanted to watch with him, and he said, "I'm not watching your movies if there are guns and violence." I continue to wholeheartedly be-lieve that we will one day watch all of the following movies together:

Movies Myles Will Like, But Do Not Yet Seem Appropriate.
Moulin Rouge, *Animal House*, *Rushmore*, *Rocky Horror Picture Show*, *Fast Times at Ridgemont High*, *The Blues Brothers*, *Raising Arizona*, *Priscilla Queen of the Desert*.

Movies Myles Will Likely Hate Under Any and All Circumstances.

District 9, Terminator, Blade Runner, Die Hard, The Bourne Ultimatum, Short Cuts, Deadman.

Movies That I Think Will Give Myles Some Insight Into Where and How I Grew Up.

Dazed and Confused, The Squid and Whale, Brother's Keeper, Running On Empty.

Movies That I Saw With My Dad When I Was Myles Age so He Has to See Them With Me Whether He Wants to or Not.

The Warriors, Alien.

Movies I Watched Lying in Bed with My Old Roommate Avi.

The Godfather I and *II.*

Movies That Have to Be Included Because Matt Dillon Has to be on the List Somewhere.

Drugstore Cowboy.

Movies That Would Seem to be Required if He is to Understand The World, Though Given The World He's Growing Up in May Be Required Less Than I Think.

Hoop Dreams, Boys Don't Cry, Bowling for Columbine, The Believer, Brokeback Mountain, City of God, Bloody Sunday, Platoon, Once Were Warriors, Deadman Walking,

The Hurt Locker, American History X, Mysterious Skin, Do The Right Thing.

Movies That Make Me so Nostalgic for High School That I Want to Force Myles to Sit Through Them Even Though We Didn't Go To High School Together.

The Breakfast Club, Heathers.

Movies that Regardless of Quality are Violent and Funny in Ways I Choose to Embrace.

Goodfellas, Pulp Fiction, Midnight Run.

Movies That Say Something About Being a Male, Even if It's Not Clear if What They're Saying is Helpful.

Punchdrunk Love, Glenngary Glen Ross, Before Sunset, The Last Seduction, Swingers, Clerks, Apocalypse Now, In The Company of Men, One False Move, Wonder Boys, Get Shorty.

Movies That My Father and I Did Not Get to Watch Together Before He Died, So Myles Has To.

Ghost Dog: The Way of the Samurai.

Movies Starring Raging Anti-Semites That I Wish We Could Watch Together, but Will Not Under Protest.

Mad Max.

I Am Your Father

I thought I might start this piece in the following way:

Hi, my name is Ben T. and I watched *Star Wars* twenty-five times when I was ten years old.

But that seems too writerly, right?

I think so, so let me say this: *Star Wars* is a touchstone for me, maybe even the touchstone for understanding my childhood, and even more so as a parent. Watching it is one of my favorite memories, and yet as popular as it was, it also represents how different I was at one time, before I molded myself into something else, something more conformist, and something that involved moving away from comic books, *John Carter —Warlord of Mars*, and movies like *Star Wars*, instead choosing to focus on becoming a varsity athlete, getting high, and chasing popular girls.

And while I may have just outgrown whatever *Star Wars* had once meant to me—escape, and possibility, lately, as I find myself drawn back to those touchstones, and the weirdo, fanboy energy I tried so hard to distance myself from, I wonder what I gave up along the way.

I also find that I am having a battle with myself about

who I am now, who I was, and who I will be, all of which plays into being a parent as well.

For one, it's me wanting Myles and Noah to want to experience these movies because they meant so much to me and I want them to mean something to them, something that will allow us to connect in some fashion, but also because watching the *Star Wars* movies might give them more insight into why I do the things I do, and maybe not now, but later, when they're trying to figure out what who I was means to who they are, and will be.

Maybe most importantly though, I want them to understand, that they can be anything they want, that they can embrace this, and that being different is fine, if not now, eventually. But that it isn't easy. It can be painful, even tortured, and while I would rather that they didn't have to feel this way at all, there's no way around it.

And that's the thing with my feelings about Myles especially. He is different, awesome and beautiful, but different, not yet fitting in, nor finding his people.

There was the time of course when Myles had a friend over who wanted to build a vast city across our living room, and Myles suggested it would be cool if they also created a parade full of circus performers to march down Main Street and the kid looked at him like he was crazy.

There was also the time that some kid from theater class said he would come over so they could run their lines, but despite Myles' repeated efforts to rehearse, the kid only wanted to play Wii Resort the entire time he visited.

I don't know whether these play dates were rougher for Myles or me, but I do know that my inclination is to protect him from situations like this and let him know that it's okay to want what you want and be who you are, and how later, it will serve him well, he just needs to get through now. But I also want to let him know that I understand what he's going through, something I want to believe is true, hence, my need to watch *Star Wars* with him.

Well that, and *Glee*.

Myles may be as big fan of *Glee*, as I was of *Star Wars* when I was his age, and while he wants to know everything about the show's storylines, including the character's back stories, their loves and hates, who's dating who, and on and on, one thing he became particularly fixated on when he was younger, was why season one had been split into two halves.

This kind of fixation on schedules and structure, is not odd for him, it might even be a sign of a genius, something parents like to tell themselves when they are concerned about their children's otherwise obsessive behaviors, but still even by his standards we talked about this quite often.

How often, you might ask? Maybe every day for a while.

Myles was also a big fan of Lady Gaga at the time, and he got very excited when he learned there would be an episode dedicated to her music.

On the way to school the morning after the Gaga episode, I decided that *Glee* had presented me with the opportunity to talk about being different, and what that might mean to him.

"Look," I say, "it's really cool that *Glee* picked the music, and stylings, of Lady Gaga, and it makes sense that they would because she's very popular, but that's not the only reason they probably chose her."

No response.

I continued on though despite the no response, because that's another thing parents do, when they decide something is a teachable moment, they make that moment happen regardless of their child's interest in what we have to say.

"So, yeah," I continue, "another reason they chose the music of Lady Gaga is because she represents being different, and how it's okay to be different than the norm, and that we can, and should, celebrate being different, or weird, because being different is awesome in all its own way. Does that make sense?"

Again, no response, Myles does not say a word, and I look for a sign that he is digesting what I'm saying, considering the implications and possibly even trying to decide how he will express not only his profound gratitude for the insights I've offered him, but my use of pop culture as a currency that speaks to him at a moment in his life so fraught with implications for growth and healthy development.

Parents love this kind of shit, kids, maybe less.

Then Myles speaks.

"So why do you think they split the season into two halves?" he asks.

"Really?" I say.

Nothing.

"So you're not going to acknowledge what I said, huh?" I reply.

More nothing, no expression, not even a knowing smile that indicates that he has no intention of acknowledging what I've offered. But he gets it, he really does, and it will clearly have a long term positive impact on his development as a man and citizen as he builds a bridge towards what will be a bright and successful future.

So we instead talked about the recent emergence of the half-season in network television, and I vow to do this better next time there is a chance to do so.

Which brings us back to *Star Wars*, and more specifically, *The Empire Strikes Back*, not that everything doesn't, right? And no, you don't need to answer that. I know it does.

One night, Myles, Noah and I watch *Star Wars* and after that they talk nonstop about watching *The Empire Strikes Back*. I know I need to find a copy before the moment passes, and when I see a chance to borrow it from the library, I grab it.

They are mostly engaged, Noah more so, waiting, waiting, waiting for Yoda, and Myles watches it, but not exactly, constantly asking the kinds of questions he tends to ask.

"When are they going to freeze Han Solo? That's this one isn't it? Does being frozen in carbon hurt? Also, do they know how much Boba Fett sounds like Boba Fat?

And why hasn't anyone made *Star Wars* into a musical? That's stupid."

Eventually, the training scenes between Luke and Yoda begin, and they soon reach the part where Yoda encourages Luke to enter this tree, which leads to a fight with Darth Vader, or at least the semblance of Darth Vader.

It's all in Luke's head, but they do fight, and when Luke defeats him and removes Vader's mask he sees his own face. The kids don't really react to this. It's as if they see that kind of thing all the time. Which they don't, right? Which is very annoying, and though I try to accept it, I still find myself feeling, and acting, like my dad, "Did you see that, and how fucked up it was?"

There is nothing, however. No reaction from either of them, but then I think, this is the teachable moment I've been waiting for, and it's not like I plan them, they just happen. Which I suppose is what every annoying parent everywhere in the universe says to justify their behavior.

But there I am, so wrapped-up in the kids, especially Myles, my very own Jedi warrior, who I believe is at battle with himself, his destiny, his father, and who he will become.

It doesn't immediately occur to me that I might be projecting my own personal battles onto Myles, the battles with my own past, who I am, and how that impacts the kind of parents I want to be for him and Noah.

But it becomes clear as I continue.

"Myles," I say, "do you see how they're showing that Luke Skywalker is in essence fighting himself, that he is in conflict about who he is, and who he might yet be?"

Nothing, and like our walk to school I look for some-thing, a reaction, some kind of movement, even a twitch, around his jaw or eyes, anything, but there is nothing, just that same beautiful fucking face I've been staring at all of these years.

"So, do you get that?" I ask, more determined, be-cause this is our moment, both of us, and I don't under-stand why he refuses to see it. "Does that speak to you in any way?"

Again, nothing, not at first, but then after a moment, Myles looks at me really seriously, and I'm waiting, and I'm wondering what profound thing he is going to say.

"So when do Luke and Princess Leia realize that even though they've been kissing they're actually brother and sister?" he asks me.

"Do you want to respond to my comment first?" I ask, hoping, thinking that the scene must have had some kind of impact.

"No," he says smiling, "when do they find out?"

"Soon," I say. "It's all coming soon."

Lost in Space

When Noah is born the pediatrician doing rounds spots a small dimple in the cleft of his buttocks and tells us to follow up on it at his one-week check-up.

"You want to be able to see the base of it," our pediatrician says, "because you don't want it to be some cavity that goes all the way to the spine."

We don't discuss this all week. In fact, we barely remember the conversation. There are now two of them at home. We are exhausted. Who thought this was a good idea?

Some people we no longer know apparently.

Still, while we may now hate ourselves, we like our pediatrician a lot. She has a big smile, she listens, she answers our endless stream of questions, and she always exposes her generous cleavage for us, which at times like this serves as a needed distraction.

We need her to tell us that Noah is fine though, but she doesn't.

"There is some hair in the dimple," she says, "that's a red flag, you should have this looked at today. I'll order a sonogram for you."

I try not to acknowledge that the sonogram technician is awfully young, not that this matters, exactly, but when you have no idea what's going on, even the semblance of experience can be reassuring, and this woman looks like she is skipping her high school classes to help us out.

I also try not to acknowledge that there is some poop in Noah's diaper when she removes it for the sonogram. Not that this matters exactly either, it just means that we're bad parents, and as we are bad parents, that means that the sonogram is now destined to go poorly.

"What do you see?" we both ask breathlessly.

"I don't know," she says, "that's not what I'm trained to do."

She's not? Who is? we wonder.

Apparently the person trained to do so is a pediatric neurosurgeon, because that is who we need to meet with next. We also need to so immediately.

We had no idea this had anything to do with neuro-surgery, then again, we don't necessarily know what it is neurosurgeons do. But it must be scary. It is scary. We were talking about butt dimples just hours before, and now our heads are starting to hurt just from the thought of going to this appointment that can't be scheduled a week from now, not even a day from now, it must be now. A sonogram is a nuisance, like poop in a diaper, but this appointment could mean surgery or something even worse, not that we have any idea what worse is.

The neurosurgeon looks like a prep school teacher, with his brown parted hair, glasses, and absentminded gaze.

"He moves his legs, right," he says, "and has normal bowel movements?"

"Yes, why?" we ask.

"It looks like he has a cyst on his spine," the doctor says. "It could be liquid and shrink on its own. It could also be a ball of extra skin. We call that a tumor, though it is not cancerous. The fear is that the cyst could tether to the spine and affect its ability to descend into the spinal column."

"So, what do you do?" we ask.

Debbie and I have spent a lifetime consciously and unconsciously crafting a relationship and narrative for ourselves grounded in the idea that we are two individuals who found love and keep it alive while still remaining individuals. But none of that applies now. Now we are one, we are Wonder Twins, power activated, form of a cyst destroyer, or whatever actual scientific term applies.

"We need to get an MRI," the neurosurgeon says ignoring our Wonder Twin power awesomeness, "so we can get a better look at it, but we can't do that until he's two months old."

"And what if it is something?" we ask.

"We'll remove it. He would have to stay in the hospital on his back for five days, but he will be fine," he says.

"Are there ever any fatalities during that surgery?" we ask.

"No, not in this country," he says. "In some foreign countries I guess."

If parenting is overwhelming enough when nothing special is going on, it feels near impossible to tackle when mired in anxiety. Given this, Debbie and I tacitly agree that we can either obsess over all that might be wrong or we can act as if we know everything is fine.

We choose the latter and do not to talk about the MRI unless we have to. Cyst or no cyst, we have to focus on taking care of Noah, Myles, and each other.

"Do you want to go for a run after dinner," Debbie says one night.

I never get out at night these days, too much kid and too much bedtime.

"Yeah?" I say.

"You could blow off some steam," she says.

"That sounds amazing," I say, "and you should go get a massage. How long has it been?"

"I don't know, forever," she says. "Or we could all go take a walk, get out of the house as a family."

"We could," I say. "We should, anything."

And so it goes for two months.

The night before the MRI, Myles is recovering from a nasty stomach virus and Debbie is battling one, the two of us up until after midnight. Debbie goes to sleep on the couch and I go in to feed Noah at 3:00 am because he is not allowed to eat after 4:00 am. As I'm finishing-up, I hear Myles wake-up and I go into the living room. I assume he has had a nightmare.

"Dude," Debbie says, "Myles has vomited all over his blanket, our blanket, and the carpet in the living room."

I clean the rug. I do the laundry. I pack Noah's bag. I go

to Walgreen's to get Gatorade and white rice. When I get home at 7:00 am it's time to go to the hospital.

I have gotten two hours of sleep.

Is this a bad dream? No, it's just parenting, I tell myself. Nothing more, nothing less.

"You cannot believe how scared I was all the time, after you got your license," my mother once said to me. "I don't think I ever quite fell asleep until I heard you walk in at night."

"When did that stop?" I asked her.

"Stop?" she said incredulously. "It never stops."

And so there's that.

When we get to the hospital, I can't fathom how a two-month old who is still battling colic is going to lie down calmly for an MRI. I also wonder if there is poop in his diaper, something we have proven is a very real possibility.

As we sit there, I quickly realize that poop is not going to be the problem. Noah has crud around his nose, and a big booger stuck there as well.

The nurse notices it too.

"I am going to get rid of that," she says.

She proceeds to put on gloves, grab a non-scented wipe, and attempts to gently massage the booger out of his nose.

It won't move.

When I am in her position, I wash my hands and then pluck the boogers out with my fingertips. I want to suggest she do this as well. I also want to do it myself. I realize that this is my anxiety speaking, and my need to control, something, anything, while I am otherwise freaking out.

As I watch her work on Noah's nose, I realize she is feeling like I am.

She doesn't want to be here and potentially find out that a two-month old baby has a problem with his spine that requires surgery and a potential array of nasty outcomes.

I sit back and she gets the booger free, smiling triumphantly in the process.

Before I know it, Noah has been packed into the MRI machine, with its loud whirrs and beeps, rolled out again, and we have been sent to the neurosurgeon for our follow-up consult.

As we travel from one building to the next, Noah falls asleep and stays asleep, one less thing to deal with, much less to feel anxious about. It will just be me and the neurosurgeon.

The neurosurgeon doesn't come, however. Instead, he sends his resident.

The resident is very handsome with closely-cropped hair, and very young, and I am reminded that everyone seems young lately. Which must say something about how not young I feel, yet another benefit of parenting.

"My wife had to stay home" I say, "but she would like to listen in by speakerphone."

"I would prefer to speak to her separately," he says.

He's calm and polite, but I wonder whether this preference to speak to Debbie separately is because the news is bad.

He begins to tell me about their concerns, and why an MRI was necessary. I tell him that I know these things. What I don't know are the results of the MRI and what the future holds. He doesn't respond to this. He goes on to talk about the medical conditions one might face in a situation like this, and I begin to feel ill. After he has gone on for some time about how Noah could end-up paralyzed I start to wonder how bad the news will be. I also wonder whether I am going to need to punch him in the face if he doesn't tell me what he knows soon.

This reminds me of the time when Debbie took the then experimental nucleofold test early in her pregnancy with Myles. The test can predict the likelihood of various chromosomal abnormalities, and as we sat there and the doctor slowly explained the thinking behind the test, as well as, what it might predict, my anxiety grew to the point where I considered grabbing him by the lapels and insisting that he tell us the results immediately, or I would be forced to punch him in the face.

Everything was fine that time. That doctor had ultimately just liked to hear himself talk about the amazing research he was doing. But is that the case today as well, because it doesn't feel like it, not now, and not yet anyway.

"Excuse me," I finally say, "but if it's bad news, can we please call my wife so we can hear it together?"

"It's not bad news," he says. "It's good news. There is nothing there at all. There never was."

"Nothing," I say.

"It's just a normal space in the spine," he continues, "but with sonograms you can't tell whether something is filling the space or not, so we presume there might be."

"So, that's it?" I say.

"That's it," he says.

There was an empty space and the doctors had to fill it, it's what they do. Parents of course do the same thing. You see that there is an empty space in your life and you want to fill it. You have a child and then you see that they also have empty spaces in their lives and you try to fill those. Maybe its soccer or art, or maybe it's another sibling.

Sometimes those empty spaces get filled with anxiety if you're not sure how your life, or your child's, is going to turn out, and other times the space is filled with fear, because it's all so unwieldy and so many bad things seem to happen so often.

There is joy as well, of course, but regardless, you never quite know what you're looking at, or what the right decision is. You can hide from these decisions of course, or you can run from them, but ultimately you have to try and figure it out, you have to hope for the best, and most of the time, like this time, you find out that all of your fears and anxieties were in your head, and it is time to move on to the next thing.

Sound Like Sleep

Myles is at a sleepover. He hasn't been on many, but he is at one tonight, and he cannot sleep. So I won't either. Not at first.

I know this, because he has called and we are on the phone.

His breath slows. Long. Steady. Full of pauses. I listen for a break. Words. My name. A sense of panic or disruption. There is nothing, though, just his breath, and what may just sound like sleep.

One minute then two. I do not breathe. Or move. I just lie there cradling the phone by my ear. Three minutes becomes five, then ten, and I decide fifteen minutes is the magic number. If I can make it to fifteen minutes, I can go to sleep myself.

Twelve minutes. Thirteen. Fifteen. Nothing.

I hang up the phone. I lay my arms across my chest, breathe in and out, and close my eyes, focusing on being calm, and taking a moment to savor this victory, though only for a moment, because I can't jinx it, the phone could ring again, and then what?

I don't want to think about it.

I know the monster that falling sleep itself can be, that my father referred to sleep as the enemy, and that maybe the inability to fall asleep is a family trait.

Unlike my father, I have always preferred to quote Nas when it comes to sleep. As in it is "the cousin of death," but that may not be so accurate. I don't fear sleep, and I don't worry that sleep is too similar to death to embrace or befriend it.

I rarely think about death at all.

Well, I rarely did before my father died and I began tussling with his ghostly presence at every turn. Or before I became a father myself and started trying not to think about death and all the irrational ways my children might face it—childhood Leukemia, porch parties, school shootings, errant cabdrivers, IEDs, and on, and on, and on.

Back to sleep though.

We let Myles cry himself to sleep like people do, some people anyway, people like us, the ones who don't believe in the family bed, and who want their rooms to offer some respite from parenting, more sanctum than love-in.

Which now that I'm actually writing this, it sounds judgmental, doesn't it?

It's not supposed to, I don't think, because all that's fine with me if it works for other parents. It just wasn't going to work for me, for us, I who couldn't sleep for such a long time, and wasn't going to add any additional hurdles to that battle. Not more than necessary anyway.

The first night he cried for one hour. We lay in bed, both of us staring at the ceiling.

"Can he die from this," Debbie says, "can you cry your-self to death? Do you think he's hurting himself?"

"No. No to all of that," I say, but I don't know, you never know, you trust, and you hope you're correct.

"Should we hug him?" Debbie asks. "What if he gets traumatized?"

"He won't," I say, and I believe this.

So we continue to lie there and this is now on me as it has been once before.

In the beginning, he had colic. He could cry fifteen to twenty hours a day. He sometimes passed out from lack of breath. He could not be soothed, would not be soothed. And he did not nap. Not ever. He might fall asleep on one of our chests from time to time during the day, but that was only as good as our ability to not move or breathe.

He would eventually fall asleep at night though, and when he did, he was so worn out from being awake and crying all day that he would sleep for four to five hours at a time during some murky stretch around midnight, when only he, us, and the people leaving the bars on Division were still awake.

"Lay him on his stomach," our Yoda-like pediatrician told us. Assuming Yoda was female and had a short, tight Afro.

We cringed.

You don't lay babies on their stomachs. SIDS, yo. Come on. Not that we said that. We just thought it, that's all. But even thinking it was enough.

"It's okay," she said. "Promise."

"But couldn't he die?" we squawked.

"The odds of that happening compared to what you're going through, is worth the trade-off," she said. "Lay him on his stomach. He will feel relief and he will sleep, promise."

We didn't do it though, couldn't, until we did. Or, I did anyway.

It was so late, and he was so up, crying, purple, and sweating.

Babies sweat you ask? They do. It's amazing, though so much more preferable to discuss long after the fact and from a comfortable distance.

Debbie was asleep.

I wondered if I should ask her what she thought about laying him on his stomach. I also wondered if I should just lie him down and allow her to not be complicit in his likely death.

I didn't wake her.

Instead, I put him down on his stomach. There was movement, not much, a hitch and a jump, but no tears, none, nada, nothing. The silence was massive and ear-shattering.

For the next hour I checked on him, never sure he truly was breathing, nor trusting he would continue to. At some point, I dozed off.

Four hours later I awoke. He was still asleep. He was not dead. I savored it for the 30 seconds I was allowed to do so. Then he was awake and he was screaming.

And here we are again.

Myles cries for an hour as we lie there in bed, but then he stops, like he's supposed to, and he sleeps. The next night he cries for only thirty-two minutes, and yes I remember the exact amount of time. I have to. It's been burned into my memory for all eternity. The third night he cries for four minutes, and then not again, like "they" promised, whoever "they" are.

I don't think my parents had to let me cry myself to sleep. I was never brought into their bed and never ventured into their room. And later, when I could not sleep, at all, anywhere, at home, at my grandparents' apartments, or at sleepovers, as the dread would build, and the endless thoughts were swirling around in my head, I never tried to find them or call them. I'm not sure I thought I was unwelcome, I just didn't think I was allowed to. Bedtime was bedtime. There were rules, even if I did live in a home without many at all otherwise.

We had a year of sleep.

A colleague once told me that as soon as you become accustomed to your child's sleep patterns they will change them. She is divorced now. Her husband left home and married someone younger who, and from what I can ascertain, doesn't want children.

Myles stopped sleeping again though. Done, totally, and he could get out of bed now and wander the house, murmuring to himself, defiant, sleep the enemy, his and ours.

Another colleague of mine told me this was a sign of genius. She also told us to get a child lock for the inside door knob in his room. It seemed cruel, bad parenting writ large, like those kid leashes you see people using at the mall or zoo.

Which is not to say those parents don't look less stressed than everyone else, it's just that they are using child leashes, which doesn't sound or look right, does it?

We held off for a month, then two, then like Piper being placed in solitary, we lost our minds a little. Well at first we lost our nights, television, conversation, the ability to walk around the house or breathe, because either he was up or we were at risk of waking him up, which is like a kind of prison, or at least an episode of *Orange is the New Black*.

We got the lock.

He cried. He cajoled. We grimaced. We cried. Sleep returned.

My father didn't sleep. I didn't know this when I was little, but later in high school, and then on into college, whenever I came home late at night he was always there on the couch, reading *Artforum* or *CINEASTE*. Sometimes we spoke. Other times not. And when I saw *Running on Empty* and watched the scene where River Phoenix comes home to find Judd Hirsh sitting on the couch, not sleeping, pensive, but welcoming, I felt I had come home as well.

It seems extreme of course to describe my father's inability to sleep, then mine, and now Myles' as a family curse. Families suffer from greater, more horrific conditions like Huntington's disease, always knowing that no matter what they do, it's likely, and untreatable, generation after generation. Our inability to sleep might not even qualify as a pattern. But there is a symmetry and the real curse is anxiety, sleep merely a symptom of having too many voices in our heads, too many fears, and too much failure as artists, men, fathers, husbands, and sons.

I would like to do better by Myles and release him from our collective fate. But that's the problem when something isn't an actual curse, there is no spell to cast or potion to brew. All we have is hard work, therapy and tools, and what happens when all of that isn't enough?

We soon entered what shall now ever be known as the "Gumpy" Era.

No door could hold Myles. No tears could be cried out. But there was a pattern. At some point every night, he would lie down on the floor at the foot of our bed with a pillow and his Disney "Grumpy" blanket, which he had started leaving on the floor in our room.

We were generally asleep when he joined us, but not always.

Regardless, I was never quite asleep enough, as I waited for him to say, "Where's Gumpy?"

He wouldn't lie down until the Grumpy patch was on the right corner of the blanket near his head. But he could never find it, ever. Some nights he might repeat the phrase "Where's Gumpy?" fifteen to twenty times before one of us moved to help him locate it.

There is an episode of *One Day at a Time* where Ann,

the single mom, and Schneider, the quasi-dashing handy man talk about sleepless nights, how they both stay up and count the tiles on their ceiling in their rooms. It is a moment of connection, a communion even. They have this in common, and because of that they can bond, if for no other reason but that one.

The thing is, they cannot sleep because they are alone. Sleep is not the enemy, isolation and the anxieties that surround it are. It is the lack of touch, love, and intimacy, and the voices that keep reminding you just how alone you are in the world and what a failure you have become. I didn't understand that at ten, but I now recognize this is what we had in common, not the lack of sleep per se, but all the reasons we cannot.

"You are in charge," the therapist says.

He is white-haired and rumple-suited. His waiting room is post-card sized, but as required by *New Yorker* stories everywhere, always playing NPR. We are seeing him because we cannot reclaim our room and we are broken.

Broken takes on many forms. The lack of sleep and accompanying anger and frustration has not led to snappy comments, belligerence, and strains in the marriage, but we don't know what to do, and we've given up, and in that way we are not whole, or healthy, we need to be fixed, and that is why we are here.

The therapist's message is clear. Myles is in charge, not us, and we need to correct that.

Which we will over many months, then years, by marching him back into room at all times of night, and repeatedly at that. We will also learn to somehow stay relaxed when he storms out of his room, full of rage and performance, his head spinning, the thoughts and anxieties bouncing around his brain so rapidly they are going too fast to control or corral.

We will sometimes help him manage this with patience and love, striking the right combination of words and firmness. Other times, many times, we will yell, and threaten, and we will hate ourselves for being so weak. But it will mostly stop, just as these things do, as new patterns form and un-form, and new challenges present themselves.

When my father was sick, or more accurately, when he finally got close to death, he began sleeping all the time. He was full of fatigue and poison, and his body, then mind began to desert him. At the very end, he slept uneasily for days, agitated and full of grimace and twitch. Then he died, just like that. One minute he was lying there as I sat next to him, and the next minute, the heavy breathing that had dogged him for his final days abruptly stopped, and he was calm, silent, sleep no longer the enemy.

Myles goes on sleepovers now, not often and not without fear. What if he can't fall asleep, or worse, what if the other kid, or kids, who vowed to stay up with him, go to sleep and he is alone with this thoughts and there are no parents, his parents, or anywhere to bounce around, available to him?

What then?

So far, despite the anxiety on all sides, the sleepovers have mostly worked, but not tonight, tonight is different, tonight he calls at 1:30 am.

"I can't fall asleep, what should I do?" he asks calmly.

"Turn on the T.V.," I say.

"I can't, I'm sitting here in the dark, and I'm not sure where it is," he says, still sounding calm.

"Can you turn on the light?"

"No, I don't want to wake anyone up," he says, now slightly agitated.

"Do you want to wake up the mom?" I suggest. "She's cool."

"No, are you kidding?" he asks, no longer so calm.

This goes on for twenty minutes and several calls and I come to realize that there is no piece of advice I can give him that will work, much less that he will listen to. Nor can I cajole him into sleep, because that won't work any better on the phone than it does at home.

There is no talking him off of the ledge. All I can do is talk to him until he can't talk any longer and the ledge itself becomes a reasonable place to sleep. So I talk about the X-Men, *The Hunger Games*, *Modern Family*, *Glee*, and *RENT*, all things he loves and endlessly has questions about. And I keep talking and talking, until finally there is breathing, no words, just breathing, and I can hang-up and go to sleep myself, fitfully, but dead to the world and without battle.

The Unexamined Life

Here's what you need to know: my father is dead and Debbie and I are talking about having a baby. My father was a complicated mix of artist, teacher, activist, and world traveler, and yet despite that, he died with regrets about things he had, and had not, done. The regrets did not make the person, but coupled with his death their impact is profound for me.

We think we can escape our parents' shadows, but moving away from them, or shutting off our feelings, even their death, does not make the shadows go away.

Children are different of course. The shadows come later, but even talking about having children makes the chance for adventure seem less likely, and Debbie and I have definitely not been on enough adventures together. And yes, I know, people go on adventures when they are parents, but will we? I don't know, which makes me think even more about regret and shadows, which leaves me spinning.

It also makes me want to run away.

Not that I want to run away from the idea of parenthood or Debbie, but for at least one last time I want to think I can be someone who takes chances and can live in the moment.

Debbie is not interested in any of that.

"Go, go somewhere I have been," Debbie says, supportive, though maybe hedging her bets a little, "but go, and then come back, cool?"

Cool.

To recap, my father is dead, we are going to have a baby, there are regrets and shadows, and I think we need an adventure, Debbie does not, and here we are.

Here being Milan.

I can head directly to Venice, which is technically my first stop, but the cheap tickets involved flying into Milan and I want to see it. I want to see everything. So I wander around, eat paninis, and stop at one church after the next. The light is brilliant, the women are beautiful, and there is a moment where I think, this is enough, I did it, I got away, I've had this experience, and I can go home now and become a parent.

But I press on. This is just the beginning.

I head to Venice, and I assume, incorrectly as it turns out, that the hotel will not be difficult to find since it advertises itself as centrally located to both the Rialto Bridge and St. Mark's Square.

An hour later it is dark, I am chilled to the bone, and I am meandering through the twisty alleys and side streets of a city I don't even vaguely know my way around and, wondering whether the hotel, or street it is supposed to be on, even exists.

During my search it strikes me just how alone I am on this trip. I have no one to express my fears to. There is no one on the streets to ask directions. And the one phone call I am able to make to what I think might be the hotel gets lost in translation as I have no idea what the person is saying and they clearly have no idea how desperate I am to find them.

Being alone is great when you want to write or dictate your own schedule. Being alone is just plain lonely when you're lost.

Later, much later, and long after this trip, when at least one child is always in the apartment when I get home from work, I have to run with a baby jogger because there is rarely the opportunity to run by myself, and Debbie and I have to negotiate for free-time, I will better appreciate how great it was to briefly have thoughts and head space that were my own, as scared and lonely as those thoughts may have been. But that is still a long way off, and again, way after I turn down what I believe is the same alley I have walked down repeatedly and my hotel is sitting there, right where it should be.

Venice may be known for things like the Titian's at the Accademia and the Pollock room at the Peggy Guggenheim, but it is the city itself that endlessly captivates. The streets twist and turn and constantly intersect. Where there are no streets, there are canals and bridges of all sizes. Water is everywhere, as are countless alleys, piazzas, and ancient buildings, many of the latter emerging from the canals like ancient concrete sea monsters.

Tradition holds that when you feed the pigeons in St. Mark's Square, they will come to you in a swirling cacophony of wings, beaks, and shrieks. Which they do, though while it is fantastically entertaining, it is also much scarier than I anticipated. I may have intended to run from regret on this trip, but I hadn't planned to be so scared while doing so.

I know this experience is a metaphor for the adventure to come, that parenting is going to be scary at every turn. Which I suppose may be obvious when written down like this, but it hadn't occurred to me until I was so far from home, and so unable to do much about these feelings.

On the flip side, a subtle shift begins to happen in Venice as well. Maybe it's the Pollacks or the pigeons, quite possibly it's the gondola ride I take on the Grand Canal as darkness falls, something just completely overwhelming in its silence and beauty, but whatever experience it is, I realize that everything I see, I now also hope to one day see through the eyes of my still unborn child. A flip has been switched, and it's not going to get un-switched, and so now I wonder how that child, or children, will experience the things I am seeing, whether they will like them or hate them, and how much I will become my dad, beseeching them to love something because it's so amazing, yet flabbergasted that they can't see it in the same way I do?

And speaking of which, I am soon seated at a restaurant in Florence and next to me, two men with wild hair and Oxford shirts are wildly gesticulating with their hands, their voices rising as they engage in a conversation so animated I wish I knew Italian.

I cannot follow what they are saying though, and so I decide to lose myself in an artichoke omelet instead. Moments later, fully lost in the omelet's buttery wonder I fail to realize that one of the gentlemen has been trying to get my attention.

"Excuse me, American, no?" he says.

"Yes," I reply wondering what local mores I have trampled on.

"What does this *Castaway* mean?" he asks.

This is not exactly what I am expecting, and I do my best to explain.

"It's kind of like being thrown away by life," I say.

He nods.

"So what did you think?" I ask.

The man pauses.

"A good movie, but not great cinema," he finally says.

As he turns back to his friend, I don't know what is harder to grasp, the irony of discussing a movie about a man adrift, or that I am discussing said movie with a man who reminds me so much of my father.

My father and I endlessly talked movies, but we will never do so again. He will never say to me for example, "How many masterpieces does someone need to make," when I ask him what's happened to Martin Scorsese's ability to make good movies. Nor will he ever see *Ghost Dog: The Way of the Samurai*, and how is that possible?

Fuck.

On the other hand, with children I at least have the chance to repeat this dynamic in some fashion. There's no guarantee they will be interested in anything I want them to be interested in, but there's a chance, and that's more than I can say about my relationship with my father.

The next morning I am walking through the Accademia and moving along somewhat perfunctorily when I am stopped dead in my tracks. I am face to face with the *David* by Michelangelo, and I am spellbound, lost in its every curve and ripple. It's so much bigger than I expected and so powerful looking. It practically glows.

I may be falling in love.

I move behind the David to see it from just one more angle, and when I do I find myself spellbound all over again. Hanging from the David's hip is easily the longest cobweb I have ever seen in my life. It floats there ethereally, silent and beautiful, swaying to and fro, light and dust dancing around it like stars at dusk. Transfixed by the cobweb's undulations, I am left with the following thoughts: first, how love can be so fickle and fleeting? And second, how can't it be someone's job to worry about such things?

A therapist once said to me that I was a good storyteller, but he didn't mean it as a compliment. What he meant was that I told stories about how I wanted to see myself instead of exploring my actual feelings. Is this trip any different, and what about my experience of seeing the David? Was seeing that cobweb as profound as I imagine it to be, or do I need it to be, adding texture to a story that I have no choice but to write, because I have no choice but to write about it, if not during the trip exactly, then someday down the road?

I can already see where I am engaging in a certain amount of myth-making about this trip, describing in my notes the person I have convinced myself I am or wish I could be. But it is not the truth. I have constructed the world as I would like to see myself in it, cool, relaxed, and able to comfortably manage the idea that having a child is scary, or that my father can go and die, and at some reasonable point I can move on, because it's time, and I have mourned enough.

I imagine that the falsity of all this will be as obvious to the reader as it now is to me, and even in my note taking, I force myself to dig deeper, searching for the places where the darkness and confusion reside. I only hope that I can continue to do so long after the trip.

I arrive in Rome during the early evening, a light rain dotting, then dripping down the lenses of my glasses, the sun just setting. The city seems so big and so empty and I am struck by how little I planned for all the loneliness and isolation that has accompanied my trip. This is, of course, what happens when you spend so little time by yourself. You don't prepare for the fact that beyond the language barriers, you don't realize just how much a constant lack of speaking and contact will begin to wear you down. Some of this is a lack of planning and vision about what I needed for the trip beyond the need for the trip, something I've never been good at anyway. When I want to do something I just do it, no research, no planning. I assume that I will somehow figure it out through sheer will and desire.

I won't be able to do this as a parent though, an act that involves all the things I haven't had to be, thoughtful about making plans, taking time to figure out how things work, and not only filtering the world through what someone else will need, but understanding those needs in the first place. I will have Debbie, and we will have each other, but what if we don't know how to do these things and never quite figure it out? What then?

I don't know. What I do know is that I cannot sit in my room and watch *Turner and Hootch* in Italian, and with that I head out in search of Trevi Fountain.

I walk along the deserted streets and I am stunned when I come upon the Via del Corso, a shopping area so teeming with people it feels more like a flash flood. I eagerly dive into the crowd before me, and I am buffeted by people from all sides, propelled forward by its force, and energized by the contact.

I eventually resurface to cut through an alley that I believe will lead me to Trevi Fountain. It is so dark, quiet, and not crowded, however, that I question whether the previous moments were real or just the longings of a lonely traveler.

But then there is light.

I turn a corner and before me is an explosion of bearded, muscle-bound statues astride waves of all sizes and surrounded by columns and sea monsters that spring forth from every possible direction. I have stumbled onto Trevi Fountain and it is larger than life.

I sit before it, and I try to take it all in, bathed in the streetlights and drizzle, and lost in its sheer audacity. It's magical really, and as I sit there soaking it all up I am reminded once again of why we travel in the first place, to be lost in something so different than the life we know, as if we have entered another world completely. I feel as if I could leave Rome that night if I had to, satisfied and complete, but if I had I would have missed my night Piazza Navona.

I wasn't even looking for it. I was just heading somewhere, and there it was, this sprawling piazza, full of cobblestones, balconies, churches, cafes, fountains, and people, people everywhere, leather-wearing and stroller-pushing, white-robed and black, vendor and caricaturist, homeless and lover.

I settle in at the Caffe Barocco, a slight chill permeating the night air as scruffy, corduroy-wearing troubadours belt out REM tunes only feet away. Unexpectedly, a handful of young American students jam into the table next to mine. They're talking and smoking and talking and eating, and then talking to me.

"Do you want to join us?" they ask.

I am a little too excited to be hearing American voices, and yet there it is, a taste of home, all feelings of isolation gone, just like that.

They are full of questions and anxieties.

"Have you been traveling by yourself?"

"I have been traveling by myself," I say.

"Where is Trevi Fountain?"

"Trevi Fountain is really easy to find," I say, "I will tell you how to get there."

"Is it hard to get around Rome?"

"Rome will feel small in a week," I say, "and your time abroad is going to be wonderful, you will never forget any of it."

As we talk I realize that as excited as I am to talk to them, I feel protective of them as well. They have been thrown into a new culture far from home, and it's all so big, and I want to hug them so much, which is not a new feeling for me, this desire to protect people, and yet it's different than how I normally experience it too.

One of the young woman looks like Natalie Portman, and while my first inclination is to check her out, it is quickly replaced by a completely different, and new, reaction for me, the idea that if Debbie and I ever have a daughter she could very well look like this, the dark hair, the big smile, the beautiful skin, and that someday she could be living abroad in some foreign city living a life I regret never having quite lived myself, but want for the children I have yet to have.

It is wonderful, and baffling, and I see now how some regrets and some shadows dissipate merely by bringing children into the world and watching them grow and thrive and live lives of their own.

I hold onto the young Americans as long as I can, but at some point we have to part. After that it is time to go home.

The Vanilla Ice Interlude:
Three Songs to Time-Out To

There are days I am dealing with an anger that refuses to dissipate. Where I feel something cruel has transpired between Myles and Noah and I react to the repetition of such behaviors, or the abuse of power they can entail, both of which are clearly triggers of mine, and must be managed as well. But I can't always manage my anger, and when I can't, I give myself a time-out.

I step away, door closed, and I let the emotions bounce off of the walls just as they are doing in my head. I also, at times, play music, because the emotions need a place to go, and they need to be channeled, and it's possible at times like this, that music does in fact soothe the savage beast, though I haven't seen the data on that.

Data or not though, I want to share the songs that help me out during these times, even merely thinking about such times, what they represent to me, and how I get through the frenzy when it's not clear anything will work.

"They say jump, you say how high."
It may be that *Bullet in your Head* by Rage Against the Machine is self-explanatory, maybe, yes? Sometimes I

am so mad at myself, my children, and at the world, I want to punch a closet door, which I have. Not good. So at those times I choose to play *Bullet In Your Head* instead, pogoing and shadow boxing until the rage has dissipated and run its course, evaporating into the cool night air. The first time I heard the song, I was looking at several hours of work, it was late, I was dreading it, and angry that I had to be doing the work at all. The song served as both a focus and a balm, and little about that has changed since.

"I've been funny, I've been cool with the lines, ain't that the way love's supposed to be?"

At times what I need is nostalgia and false hope. Would the world of *Mad Men* even exist without these things? I need to believe that life was better once and can be again. Maybe not in this exact moment, but soon, because I like to believe I remember what it was like, pre-children, when things were perfect for me. When there was no anger or confusion. When I lived in a world where Rick Springfield was God, *Jessie's Girl* ruled, and it really was okay to pine away for my best friend's girl. Back then I didn't have a family that might implode because of my actions. There was no mortgage to pay or vaccinations to worry about. Instead there was goodness, longing, lust, and Rick Springfield's great belief that not only was such longing alone more than enough to worry about, but that it would all somehow be okay.

"All right stop, collaborate and listen, Ice is back with my brand new invention."

Sometimes, of course, I must laugh, a lot, if only to stanch the flow of tears. Because when the bad feelings remain, where would I be without humor and the opportunity to recognize that some people have it worse than me? Even celebrities who have slept with Madonna still write songs like *Ice Ice Baby*, grow grungy white-boy dreads, and get hung upside down off of balconies by Suge Knight. Frankly, it feels good to gloat. It's a release, and sometimes, and this despite my best intentions, I even mouth the words to *Ice Ice Baby* because they're so damn catchy, and because despite Ice's protestations, they remind me of *Under Pressure* by Queen. All of which makes me happy, allows me to feel sane, and unlike so many other things in recent history, doesn't make me want to punch anything at all.

Which is good, very, very good, all of it, especially when that moment comes, where the frenzy is now memory, the children are smiling, and I know that I will live to see another day, or at least live long enough to see the next thing happen, because something will happen, it always does.

Anatomy of the Story

1.

Myles is five and this is how it ends.

"We cannot use it," the publisher says when I call her. "I'm sorry, this is a nonfiction anthology."

"I realize that now," I say, sitting at the kitchen table, embarrassed and sorry, but sad to see an opportunity pass when they are so few and far between.

"It's just that we cannot mislead our readers," she says. "Their emotions are so raw. It wouldn't be right."

2.

The publisher calls me about my story "The Good Parents." She wants to publish it an anthology they are working on about parents and loss.

"We love it," she says. "It's so moving, the editors were crying as they read it."

This feels like a small triumph. I have never had a piece accepted for inclusion in an anthology, but it has always seemed to me that doing so is a sign that you've made it, or will.

I am confused by the tears, but I decide to ignore that.

People editing stories about loss are bound to be more sensitive to the content of those stories as the traumas building upon themselves, and possibly cause them to relive their own traumas as well.

Later that day I am reading a story in *The New Yorker* by T.C. Boyle. The story is about a man who doesn't want to go to work and so he says his son is sick. That first lie escalates into further lies and an escalating, albeit completely fabricated, health crisis for his son, and eventually there is no way to escape his fabrications, but to tell the truth.

I spend a moment meditating on lies. I am from a family of liars, or so my mother tells me, and I have always been a great liar. In high school, when I had no rules, I lied just to see what I could get away with, which was everything. Since then I have taken the Spider-Man approach to things—with great powers come great responsibilities, and so I try to never lie at all.

Myles is a good liar as well, or a reflexive one anyway. When he was once caught with two other kids playfully beating-up another friend in the playground in pre-school, the teacher who had watched the whole thing confronted them. The other kids broke immediately and admitted everything, but Myles never did, it was a showdown, and he didn't budge, something that perversely left me full of pride and horror all at once.

Parents lie to their children and themselves all the time. And those of us who write about our families take those lies, mix them with our fears and compulsions, and bend them into a language that becomes a story. Sometimes this means that we cannot recall which details are based on actual truths and which are fabrication.

This was not a problem with the piece I submitted for the anthology though and as I read the T.C. Boyle story I realized that the editors of the anthology were crying because they thought I had submitted a true story.

I could have lied. I wanted to lie. But I called them and I told them that I had made a mistake.

3.

The waiting room at Children's Memorial is full of energy, an endless stream of sick children going 100 miles an hour and giving no sign that they are afflicted by anything worse than being stuck indoors.

Myles is three and his surgery is considered minor, maybe fifteen minutes in length, and an hour total of sedation. The doctors plan to use general anesthesia though, which makes us nervous. While everything is certain to go fine, no one can truly say what will happen during that hour or how Myles will respond.

Similarly, no one can say how skillful the doctors really are. There is a need to trust them, however, to firmly believe that they know what is best, and that they will do things correctly.

If we do not feel this way, we cannot go through with the surgery, and if we cannot go through with the surgery, what else is there to do?

And that's the catch of course. As parents, how can we know what to do, when what needs to be done is so far beyond our skill sets? We think we know what to do when Myles is bullied, and we are fairly certain, if not actually confident, about our ability to talk about drugs or what "whores" are. But surgery, the possibilities are endless and our fears of the unknown are boundless.

We are brought into the pre-op area and we are visited by Dr. O., a somewhat doughy, cherubic looking anesthesiology resident.

"How well does Myles separate from the two of you?" Dr. O. asks.

"Okay," Debbie says, "like any kid."

"It's just, we don't want to cause him any trauma going into surgery," Dr. O. says. "We know this leads to further trauma later in childhood when they have other surgeries."

"He won't be having any other surgeries," Debbie says.

Dr. O. smiles painfully.

"He will certainly have more surgery. People have surgery," Dr. O. says.

"Not me," Debbie says, "I've have only been in the hospital for my birth and his."

"Okay," Dr. O. says awkwardly, "so what I'm going to suggest is that we give him some medication about five minutes before the surgery that will induce temporary amnesia. This way he won't remember the surgery, and he won't remember you when we go back for the surgery."

This is unexpected. Induce amnesia, for a child? Would good parents approve of such a thing?

"What if the amnesia becomes permanent?" I ask.

"It won't," Dr. O. says, smiling painfully again. "It always wears off."

"Always," I say, "are you sure? Does the research show this?"

"Yes," Dr. O. says suddenly zoning out like a child does when they don't want to answer the questions before them.

"It's just that memory is so tricky," I say. "Do you really claim to understand it? People forget some things, and remember other things, and they don't know why, but you do? How does that work, I would like to know more about it."

"Do you mind?" Debbie asks, looking at me. "Can we focus on the surgery?"

Dr. O. snaps back to attention.

"Yes, okay, then, we'll be back to give him the shot in a moment, and then we will go in for the surgery, right?" Dr. O. says.

"Right," we say.

Dr. O. walks away.

"I'm sorry," I say, "I'm nervous. Getting caught up in that stuff is way better than thinking about the surgery."

"It's fine," Debbie says, "but let's not forget why we're here."

"Hello, I'm Dr. P., the chief anesthesiologist," Dr. P. says, arriving moments after Dr. O. leaves. He looks like a tri-athlete. He has gaunt cheeks, rippling forearms, and an intense stare that we both find unnerving.

"I'm going to ask you a few questions," Dr. P. continues, which he does as he begins to tap Myles' back and chest.

"Is he allergic to anything?"

"No."

"Has he had anything to eat since midnight last night?"

"No."

"Has he been sick at all?"

"He was coughing for a couple of days," Debbie says, "but he hasn't today, and didn't last night."

"Okay then," he says, not blinking, "so would you say he is the healthiest he can be, because we don't want to put him under if he isn't."

"I don't know," Debbie says, "I told them we didn't want to come in if they thought you would be unwilling to perform the surgery,"

"Sure, okay," Dr. P. says, "but is this as healthy as Myles can be?"

"Look," I say feeling the urge to punch him, but too intimidated by his broad shoulders and square jaw to truly consider doing so, "he's been coughing, so he's not as healthy as he can be. If you're asking us if he's healthy enough to have surgery, we can't answer that, and you can't put that on us. What do you think?"

"He's fine," Dr. P. says tapping on Myles' back one more time, "and I see we're going to induce amnesia, right?"

"Right," Debbie says. "Also, what about my walking

back to the operating room with him? I understand that I can do that if it is okay with you."

"You can," Dr. P. says, "but there's really no point, he won't remember you."

"I'll go back," Debbie says.

"Let me finish," Dr. P. says. "If something happens to you—you faint or you fall—there will be no one to help you. We are there to care for your son."

"I know," Debbie says, "I'm fine with that."

"Wait, let me tell you what to expect," Dr. P. says. "You may see your son shake like he's having a seizure when we put him under. His eyes may roll back in his head making him appear as if he's dead. And if he stops breathing we may have to put a tube down his throat."

"That's fine," Debbie says.

"Okay then," Dr. P. says, "when he first wakes-up after surgery he may not recognize you. He may also be inconsolable for about an hour."

"Fine," we say.

And then he is gone.

A nurse walks up moments later to give Myles his shot.

"This is the shot for the amnesia," the nurse says, "I'm sorry."

She has a blonde pageboy haircut and big cheeks. She is smiling and grimacing simultaneously. She seems sincere.

"His initial reaction to the shot," she says, "will be giddiness and joy. He will look like he's intoxicated. A little preview of things to come when he gets older I guess."

I hold Myles in place and Debbie sings to him as the nurse gave him the shot.

"*The screen door slams Mary's dress sways. Like a vision she dances across the porch as the radio plays.*"

Myles shudders, cries briefly, his face momentarily contorted and red, and then he climbs into Debbie's lap. Within minutes his head is lolling about like a bobble head doll and he is smiling broadly, saying, "Mommy, Mommy," over and over again.

We laugh despite ourselves. It is just what we needed, and I think about how this is a moment we will remember for years to come.

Dr. N. comes back to prep Myles for surgery. We cover his head in kisses and nuzzle his beautiful baby neck. We tell Myles we love him and Debbie walks to the operating room with them. She is back just a few minutes later.

"Did you see anything scary?" I ask.

"No," she says, "Dr. P. blocked my view with his arm."

Hand in hand we walk back to the waiting room, wanting to be stoic, wanting to be relaxed, and wanting not to be so worried about a simple procedure.

We sit down together and idly leaf through *US Weekly*. Britney Spears is studying the Kabalah. Jennifer Aniston is looking much too thin. The Backstreet Boys are mounting a comeback. The Sox game is on and I check the score intermittently.

Time passes. Fifteen minutes becomes thirty. Thirty becomes forty-five. And there is no word on how this simplest of surgeries is going.

It is here, that my mind wanders, and I realize just how much I've been trying to control my anxiety, how a good parent wouldn't support surgery of any kind unless it was absolutely necessary to save their child's life.

This isn't such a surgery I think, and I begin to believe that Myles is dead. It doesn't matter that the surgery was easy, or common, surgery is surgery, fear is fear, and Myle's beautiful little heart has stopped. They don't know why this happened, just that it happens sometimes, like a bolt of lightning.

Despite what has now clearly gone down just down the hall, doctors and patients continue to move by us without missing a beat. The Sox game is still playing on the television screen in the waiting room. And people are endlessly shuffling in and out of their cars in the parking lot outside the window in front of us.

All of this is happening of course, because it has to, because just like when my dad died, life goes on. People will care about your personal tragedies if they know about them, but they won't care as much as you do. They can't, and they won't, and this sucks, but life isn't fair, and that's just the way it is.

I could tell you, that it is now where I force myself to take a step back and recognize that this is fear speaking, that death is not something unknown to me, that it can happen, any time, anywhere, but that doesn't mean it's truly happening now anywhere, but in my head.

But I can't do that—step away, right myself. I can't even lie to myself despite my ability to do so at will in almost any other situation. Instead, I start to write a story in my head about good parents and a beautiful child that dies too soon.

I hate to be so cliché, and yet I have no choice; I write, it's what writers do. We are immersed in our lives, which means we are immersed in our material, and at the moment, my material is fear, and death, and the idea that Dr. N. will soon come to see us and tell us that what she has to say isn't good news.

I don't finish the story, however, not then anyway, and not in any nonfiction way either, because as I sit there, lost in my head, swimming in fear, life going on around me, Dr. N. suddenly appears before us.

"It went great," she says, "and you can see him now."

4.

Myles is one and we go see Dr. M., his youngish pediatrician. She has a wonderful smile and boundless energy. She also has bountiful cleavage, which we are exposed to one V-Neck sweater after another.

"There you go, there's fluid again," she says.

"Is there anything we can do?" we ask.

"No, not really," she says. "If the ear infections start happening more closely together, you might consider tubes, but you don't need to at this time. Let's see what happens next winter."

We wait and Myles thrives. His hair became reddish brown like mine, and his laugh grows hearty like Debbie's. He has my dad's eyes, but Debbie's look—long, lean, and beautiful.

He begins pulling himself up to his feet and taking his first unwieldy steps, endlessly crashing into chairs, bookshelves, and tables. I grimace each time Myles bangs his head, and I try to take comfort in the line my mom says to me whenever I mention any kind of Myles-related mishap to her.

"Children have survived for thousands of years."

They have died for thousands of years as well I think, but I choose to ignore that.

And then Myles' fourth winter hits.

Myles is now taking a ninety-minute class with Debbie once a week at Lakeshore Prep. He has friends, he goes out more, and he starts to get sick more often. The ear infections start to arrive with a greater frequency as well. The fluid in his ears no longer dissipates between infections and Myles starts to tug on his ears after long, sleepless nights and say, "Hurt."

Doctor M. says it is time to see an Ears, Nose, and Throat specialist and recommends Dr. N. Dr. N. has black hair and sharp cheekbones. She is short and speaks fast.

"He needs tubes," she says. "It's a simple surgery, so let's go in and get it done."

We do not feel there is much choice. Actually doing something is terrifying, but at this point we mostly just want the problem to go away. Raising a child is tiring enough, and we have no energy left for illness, much less making tough decisions.

On the day of the surgery we take off from work and the three of us lay around the house watching *Willy Wonka and the Chocolate Factory* until it is time to go to the hospital.

Myles has been coughing the last couple of days, but not at all that day or the night before. We know that surgeons don't like to perform surgery when someone is sick, so Debbie calls the hospital and asks whether they should come in or re-schedule. The nurse says Myles doesn't sound all that sick and that we shouldn't worry about it.

We go in.

5.

We are good parents. We think we are good parents. We want to be good parents. We read *What to Expect When You're Expecting* when Debbie first gets pregnant, and I sing Bruce Springsteen lyrics into Debbie's stomach during the pregnancy so the baby will know my voice.

"*The screen door slams, Mary's dress sways. Like a vision she dances across the porch as the radio plays.*"

Debbie does yoga and drinks plenty of water. I cover all of the electrical outlets in the apartment and put locks on the drawers. We take classes on infant CPR and breastfeeding, and with Debbie's urging, I even sign up for a new father's class.

The baby is born on a cold, Chicago night, kicking and screaming, masses of hair flying everywhere. It is a boy and we name him Myles. We saw the name in a baby name book at a Barnes & Noble we stopped in on the way to a U2 show at the United Center. We wanted an "M" name for my father Mike, because it felt too soon, and too weird, to have another Mike Tanzer running around.

Myles with a "y" jumped out at us, the Scottish translation meaning something like "warrior of the heart," which sounded like my dad to us. Plus there are allusions to Miles Davis, which spelling aside, feels cool, and seems like a good choice of name for a baby clearly destined to be the future recipient of a MacArthur Genius Grant.

We find a level of mastery changing diapers in public bathrooms and trimming Myles' little nails without slicing the tips of his tiny fingers and toes. He has colic, but that passes. There is sleep stuff as well, but ultimately, the biggest issue at this early age is with speech, and Myles' ears, or more specifically his propensity for ear infections.

Which is how it begins.

Going Home

Nostomania: an irresistible compulsion to return home

I ran away from home once, and no, it wasn't the kind
of running away you see in those gritty movies Mark Van
Goseselaar used to make for Lifetime where he has to hus-
tle on the Los Angeles streets so he and his girlfriend can
eat, or like those times when Myles says he is going to run
away and he throws his teddy bear and a University of Illinois pillow from Dave & Buster's into his backpack, puts on
his coat, and stomps down the hall, my stomach in knots.

I never ran away as a kid. I never even had the inclination. No, I ran away from home as an adult. I did it
with Debbie's blessing mind you, and I didn't storm out.
I wasn't mad at all, I was just a little lost after my father
died, and feeling trapped by a future that involved a baby
that was yet to be born, much less conceived.

Which I suppose means I didn't really run away at all.
I just went away.

Regardless, that was a story about trying to get away
from home, and this one is not, it's the opposite really.
This one is about desperately trying to get back home, to
Debbie, to Chicago, and to a baby no longer so mythical,
though still not actually born.

September 13th—Portland, ME—6:15am EST

I am at the Greyhound station waiting for it to open, hoping that buses will be leaving Portland today, and that, if they are, one will somehow eventually get me to Boston, and then home. It's funny given how much I travel for work, and how much I enjoy it, that the urge to get home can feel just as strong as the urge to get away.

I have felt this way, of course, at the end of a long trip when it feels like it is time to finally get home, and sometimes even more so just getting to O'Hare and knowing home is but that last train ride away.

I'm not sure that I feel different this morning, but the world as we know it is different. It looks the same, maybe even feels the same, and yet, like a vague memory, there's something a little fuzzy around the edges. I am just not quite sure of what I think I know and I don't know, or when I will ever quite be sure again. Being far from home doesn't help. Even being someone who travels all the time, I am always a lot more destabilized when I am on the road. There are hotel rooms I've never seen before, and offices I've never visited, and just a whole lot of not knowing exactly where I am.

Mind you, I'm not even sure what this whole concept of home even means to me. Is it about safety, or the known, or control, or what? One reason I ask is because I never even remember thinking all that much about all of this until recently.

Of course, until recently Debbie wasn't pregnant, and while briefly leaving her has never struck me as a threat to the relationship, we are apart, and then we are together again, and that's not so confusing. But this baby is something more, this baby is tissue and fiber, and I don't know anything about how this relationship is going to work, what will break it, and what will not. I am trapped by the fear of the unknown, and with all my fears already exaggerated, I just want to get home and lay some of them to rest.

September 13th—Somewhere between Worchester, MA and Albany, NY—2:10pm EST

I got to Boston so early that a line had yet to even form at the gate to Chicago. There was a row of six empty chairs that lay perpendicular to the door and directly across from the spot where people are expected to line up. As I approached the gate I found myself talking to two English couples who were supposed to be flying to Las Vegas as part of their trip across the States.

"Why don't we take those seats?" they suggested.

My inclination was not to do so. Experience told me that the people who eventually got in line would not respect the fact that we were there first and would unquestionably look to board ahead of us.

"I don't think we should," I said. "Aren't you worried that people will try to cut us in line if we do?"

"Rubbish," they said, sitting down, and turning back to their newspapers.

I was in a bind. I wanted to go sit at the front of line, but I was worried about the message it would send. What if they thought that I was trying to cut in front of them? I sat down. I was embarrassed for being so cynical and so ready to cave in to my anxieties. Yet, while I do not want to say I now feel vindicated (okay, I do) as predicted, when the gate opened, the woman at the front of the line that had formed next to us made her move to bum rush those of us who had grabbed the seats.

Which all feels a little crazy really, because there I was not trusting the people in line, and feeling bad for feeling that way, and then they showed us that they were not to be trusted.

What am I supposed to do with that?

Meanwhile, while even on a normal day such a scenario is all so very petty and small, the question of trust, and its importance, and what it means to any of us is a particularly poignant one this week.

Picture it, I walked into a conference room to conduct a series of interviews for work, and then when I walked out a couple of hours later the first thing I heard, was hadn't I heard? Heard, heard what I asked? This person then told me that two hijacked planes had been flown into the Twin Towers and they had subsequently collapsed; a third plane had crashed into the Pentagon; and a fourth into a field in rural Pennsylvania.

Now, could I trust what had just been said, and forget whether I trusted the messenger? Was it even possible that what I had heard is what was actually said? Could I even trust myself? I walked into a room on a beautiful day, the sun shining, and the birds singing, and all that kind of stuff, and when I walked out the country was in flames. How can that be?

On top of that Debbie, six months' pregnant Debbie, had left that very morning from New York City to fly to Chicago. She had to be fine, of course, but did I know for sure? Did I know anything for that matter? I have trusted the universe to work in a certain way, and while terrorists are out there, they don't do things like this do they, and here, and on commercial flights?

Flying was scary enough already wasn't it? Did I ever really trust that I would land every time I took off? No, but I did it, because I trusted that really horrible shit just couldn't happen.

And so now what I am supposed to trust?

Further, even though I had eventually learned that Debbie had landed, baby intact, what about the next time, or the time after that? Are we going to fly with this baby, risking his or her life? Is that acceptable? Is it good parenting? And how do you know? Or, said differently, how do you know what's truly irrational, when the irrational actually occurs?

And yet, it has barely been 48 hours. Unbelievable maybe, but true. Only 48 hours since the Towers fell and planes dropped from the sky, and the world in so many ways, big, small, and otherwise, has gone on. People are at work. The highways are crowded. Starbucks everywhere are making coffee. And as we whip along the highway, blue skies above, lazy clouds lolling about, playfully really, even the leaves are starting to change.

Soon enough planes will fly and Barry Bonds will hit more home runs, because like the day we buried my father, the world goes on, the sun also rises, babies will be born, including mine, and nature gracefully, though sometimes achingly, moves on.

So yeah, what do we do about trust when time keeps moving forward regardless of our human needs and wants, and how do I explain any of this to the child I have yet to have?

September 13th—Albany, NY—3:30pm EST

As the bus had begun to fill up earlier I went through the usual Greyhound/Southwest post-getting-in-line-early, pre-leaving, cattle call anxiety-laden ritual we all go through, wondering which person coming down the aisle would choose to sit next to me.

Would it be the huge looking guy who is going to be rubbing into me the whole trip? Or the older woman who always wants to fucking talk? Or might it be the babe? And what would that mean? Why would I even want the babe to sit next to me? I'm an old married guy aren't I? Well, not old, maybe, but married for sure, and with a baby on the way.

Is it okay then to want the young blonde in the torn jeans, torn across her butt no less, and the University of New Hampshire baseball hat coming down the aisle to sit down next to me? What about when she doesn't sit next to me? Should I care about that? What was I going to do if she had chosen to sit next to me? Talk her up?

Make out with her in the wee hours of the journey?

It strikes me at this point how wonderful it is not to care as much about these things as I once did, and how freeing it is not to have worry about whether hooking up is remotely in the cards.

Of course, even as I sit here by myself, and with nothing to prove to anybody, I have to ask whether this is the truth or just another myth I am creating about what I'd like to be—the uncaring, totally cool, non-interested-in-engaging-young-women kind of happily married, baby-on-the-way guy. Because am I really that guy?

I am reminded of a flight I took some months back where a young brunette with a sweet bob-cut, black tights, and a white t-shirt had been assigned the seat next to mine. As I went into my bag for some reading material I came across a copy of *First Time Father* magazine and I decided to read it thinking that the new dad thing certainly couldn't hurt my chances to draw her into a conversation. As I pulled it out, I glanced her way, and she was just lovely, a vision really, but already sound asleep, and not to awake until we landed, where she immediately bounded into the arms of her equally attractive boyfriend.

I want to believe that I am above all of that, and I certainly want to believe that becoming a father will curb some of it, but I am starting to question whether that is accurate. If you were a dick before you became a dad, maybe all that becoming a dad means, is that now you happen to be a dick who is also a father.

Damn.

September 13th—Somewhere between Niagra Falls and Cleveland, OH—11:30pm EST

Day has become night, and night an endless stretch of highway, when the young blonde in the ripped jeans, who turns out to have a New Zealand accent (seriously) finally says a word to me.

"What could you possibly be writing about in your journal?" she suddenly says. "Nothing is happening around us. We're just endlessly driving, on and on and on."

"This is true," I say, "but every mile, and every moment really we're all experiencing something new and I'm just trying to capture all of that however little that may be."

She doesn't seem all that sold on this answer, she seems disgruntled actually, and maybe even kind of bored with our already brief conversation.

I ask her how she has found herself on the bus and after telling me how she can't get home unless she gets some money from friends in Indiana she turns away to stare out the window.

My initial reaction to this exchange is to wonder why she is so uninterested in talking to me. Is staring out the window such a better option? But as this wave of narcissism passes I am struck by the fact that my response to her question has clearly thrown her in some way.

I am also struck by the fact that here we are on this road to nowhere trying to cope with not just the length of the trip itself, but the fact that we have to be taking it at all, and maybe what her reaction is really about is how we as individuals cope at a time like this and how we maintain any semblance of control in a world not of our own making.

I choose to write and read during the trip, and if I didn't feel so desperate to get home, I might beg the driver to pull over for a half an hour so I could go for a run. Because even more than writing, or escaping into a book, when the world is spinning just a little too much beyond what I can control or make sense of, it is running that usually allows me to get by.

This makes me wonder what it will be like when the baby is actually here. Will I have time to read, run, or write? And will I write about them? Of course I will. I will have no choice about that. But what about the baby— how will he or she cope, assuming they need to at all? Because that would be cool wouldn't it, raising a child that doesn't need to cope with anything—scary things, fucked up things, traumatic things, things like violence and cancer and dead parents.

It's possible, right?

I know it's not, but for a moment why not pretend it is. Isn't there enough sadness right now anyway? Which brings me back to the girl from New Zealand. I can't run right now, so I read, and when I'm not reading, I write, and it works. But what does she have? What if her means for coping with being on bus for countless hours far from home is to act like nothing is going on? What if denial is what gets her through the day, or at least this day, and then what if I turn around and say what do you mean nothing is happening, just look around? I imagine that could fuck someone up, and when it hits me like that I find it's my turn to look out the window for a little while.

September 14th—Somewhere near Fort Wayne, IN—7:05am CST

It has been just over 24 hours since I left Portland and we're looking at maybe three more hours or so before we arrive in Chicago. Many on the bus will still have places to go even when we get there, new buses will await them, and maybe more lines as well. I slept for three hours and may not again until I'm home in my bed, with my pillow, and if I'm lucky Debbie's pregnant belly pressing into my back. It feels like we are a million miles away from where we started as we pass by cornfields, signs advertising fireworks, mist covered ponds, all hazy and eerie, and finally the first sign for Chicago I've seen the entire trip. It is at this point that I start to believe that we may just make it, but I'm not sold, not just yet anyway. Again, it's about trust, and I just don't want to trust that Chicago is as close as I want it to be.

September 14th—Chicago, IL—9:50am CST

But then fuck it all if the Sears Tower doesn't just pop up, hovering there off in the distance, past the dandelions, and the trees, and the little that remains between wherever here is and Chicago. And now it's even closer. And the Kennedy Expressway has just appeared. I've never been so happy to see it. And then the Cell, the sign out-side advertising tickets, and me having forgotten by this time that a season is still being played. Now we're bump-ing along the old South side streets, blue skies as far as the eye can see, and rickety old bridges, and factories, and self-storage facilities. Soon we're on Canal, and we're rolling by Dominick's and the White Palace Grill. We've turned onto Roosevelt, driving past Gingiss Formal Wear, and then onto Jefferson, and there's Murphy and Miller, Inc. and Grainger, and we're so in the city, we're so here, and then there's the bus station, and then we pull in.

We made it, and it's not the apartment, and there is no Debbie or that unborn baby, not yet, but fuck it if we haven't made it to Chicago.

Underwater

"I heard this kid singing at the playground," Debbie says, "He sang so well, and every word was so clear. It was amazing."

"Yeah? Cool," I say knowing where this is going.

"No, not cool," she says. "He was younger than Myles, and Myles can't do that."

No he can't, I think. This is something we both know, and have acknowledged, but haven't necessarily thought of as a problem, a real problem, another problem.

But that is clearly no longer an option, so we takes advantage of the state's free zero to three assessment program and schedule an appointment with a speech therapist.

"What are your concerns?" the woman asks.

The woman is at our house to do the speech assessment. She has long brown hair, high cheekbones, and what I think is a Croatian accent. She is also young. They are all young.

"That he doesn't talk like other kids, that we can't really understand him," we say. "And that he might grow frustrated around children who can't understand him."

"Does he seem to understand your questions and requests?" she asks.

"Yes, if we ask him to go into his room and get a diaper he knows what to do," we say.

"What percentage of his words do you think you understand?" she asks.

"Maybe 50 percent for me," I say.

"And 60 or 65 percent for me," Debbie says.

"Does he know phrases, and can he put two or more words together?" she asks.

"Yes, he will say 'what you do' or 'where you go,' things like that," we say.

"Has he had many earaches?" she asks.

"Maybe half a dozen," we say.

"Okay," she says.

She's taking notes. She smiles now and again. I'm not sure whether we are saying too much or too little. Nor am I sure if we are saying the right things, much less whether we are saying them in the right way. Meanwhile, what does her smile mean? It means nothing, nothing helpful certainly.

"Does he know the difference between boys and girls?" she asks.

We don't know, we've never asked him. Why haven't we asked? We're not sure. We're not good parents.

She shifts her attention to Myles, playing with him and asking him questions. Even though he's responsive and game for anything, I find myself continually wanting to help him say things he's struggling with. I don't want to believe he has any delays or any more challenges than are absolutely necessary. And, I don't want to keep wondering whether we are in fact capable of protecting him from the challenges that seem to keep coming at him.

When he had colic, nothing worked. Not the swing with the uterine swoosh, nor the long walks in the stroller, nothing. He cried and cried and that was that. And with his ear infections, we always seem to realize what is happening a day or two late, his suffering boundless and unnecessary.

Sometimes at the playground, I watch him struggle to share with other children. It is easy for me intervene at those times and make things right, but am I supposed to, and if so, how quickly?

"He has strong language skills," the woman says. "He understands what you're asking him to do. He knows words. His vocabulary is off of the charts. But he is struggling to close his words, and I am also worried that he might become frustrated in social situations."

"So, would you recommend speech therapy?" we ask.

"I would," she says

"What might have caused this?" we ask. "What could we have done differently?"

"I'm not sure," she says, "a child who speaks like this would have no matter what. It might have something to do with the earaches, though."

"Why the earaches?" we ask, thinking about all the times it took us a couple of days to realize he had one.

"It's like he's been underwater when you have been speaking to him, "she says.

In the essay *Me Talk Pretty One Day*, David Sedaris talks about having to attend speech therapy as a child. The speech therapist makes it her goal to get him to say a word that starts with "s" so that they can work on his lisp. He refuses to do so, doing everything in his linguistic powers to use words that are similar to those she wants him to say, but don't begin with "s." The speech therapist finally breaks down, and as she cries, she tells him that she feels like she has failed. Sedaris says, "Sorry," and the therapist smiles, before saying, "Gotcha."

Speech problems exist as one "gotcha" after another. We are all in a battle with ourselves to own language, and say things as we wish to say them. But our brains are all too happy to fail us, and when they do, we have lost something profound: the chance to express ourselves.

Learning to write is like that too, of course. Myles wanted to talk, but he was unable to form the words. I wanted to write, and while I understood the basic concepts, had ideas, and the desire, I couldn't find the right words, much less form the sentences I could picture in my head.

It turns out that Myles needs to receive a hearing test at Illinois Masonic. This had not been discussed during the assessment, and we wonder whether we should be concerned. A hearing test for a two and a half year old is a big deal, isn't it?

I don't want to be worried, nor do I want to be self-ish, but I do want Myles to be fine, and I want him to do whatever he will do as unencumbered as possible.

We go to Illinois Masonic and are greeted by the audiologist. We are led into a soundproof room with a big window. On either side of the window are speakers with stuffed animals on top of them, one a gorilla with a drum, the other a teddy bear. The audiologist stands on one side of the window and looks in on us. I sit in a chair in the back and Myles sits on Debbie's lap in a chair in front of me.

I begin to feel sick. What if something is truly wrong?

The test starts and the sounds begin. There are different tones, pitches, and volume, and Myles catches every one of them, high, low, left, or right, saying "there" and pointing in the appropriate direction each time he identifies where he has heard something.

Myles' response in turn prompts the corresponding stuffed animal to jump up and down, or clap its hands, actions I am repeatedly tempted to take myself.

After the test is over, we are informed that his hearing is fine, and we smile, breathe sighs of relief, and cover his little face with kisses. We also learn that a hearing test is considered standard procedure in a case like this.

We find a speech therapist that can come to our apartment once a week prior to work. She has a big smile and lots of energy and Myles takes to her immediately. During the first session she and Myles build a farm, working through a bag of animals that Myles has to identify. She doesn't let him settle for pointing at the animal he wants while saying something simple like "please" or "there," as we might do, but instead encourages him to properly ask for them, "Can I have the horse please?"

As I watch them I think about my efforts to become a writer. I have benefited from hard work and repetition, but I have also benefited from people telling me what sentences ought to sound like, how characters would actually talk, and that I cannot settle for what's easiest when I have the ability to push harder and deeper to express myself.

Now Myles has that chance as well.

It's very easy to beat yourself up during these sessions, and the healthy thing to do, might involve not watching them at all. But they are in the house, and they are intimate, and even when I try to convince myself I am not watching, just lingering, I intensely watch them all, hanging on each moment, exercise, and word.

Still, even finding myself so enmeshed in the sessions, it's not clear anything is happening at all until it is, because at some point Myles clearly begins to blossom. He is not only using more words and phrases all the time, but closing more words as well.

He is still struggling, but he is talking, just like that, and I am struck that this is how it works, and that there is no escaping it. We are all trying to find our voice and say what we want to say in the ways we want to say it. Sometimes these things require an intervention, and sometimes they don't, but when we push and are pushed, a voice will emerge.

Both Myles and Noah have helped me find my voice as a writer, just as David Sedaris' speech therapist helped David Sedaris find his voice. Like me, Myles' voice is still evolving, and it can be hard to see that it's happening at times, but that's because we're in it, and it's new, and we still have no idea how things are going to turn out.

The Don Draper Interlude: A *Mad Men* Guide to Raising Children

Mad Men is noted for its spot-on sense of period detail, and its exploration of gender dynamics, office politics, and identity. *Mad Men* also provides insights, however, into how we parent in this age or any other, and to prove it, I engaged in an exploration of said theory while deconstructing the lines in "The Collaborators" from Season Six. The results are startling.

"I don't think about it."

This is Don Draper's approach to affairs and spouses, and in this case with his new lover Sylvia, played by Linda Cardellini, the smart girl from *Freaks and Geeks*. It's not an admirable trait, and I suppose it implies he's dead inside, though it is also a reflection of what happens when you grow-up in a whore house, and watch your pregnant step-mother have sex with your "uncle," the head rooster, through a keyhole in a very bad pageboy haircut. This line also applies however, to parents, this parent anyway, and fears of childhood Leukemia, school shootings, porch parties, mental illness, bullying, and child sexual abuse among other things I just cannot bare to think about when it comes to my children and the world that awaits them outside of our living room. Because if I were to think about these things what then? What I would do? I wouldn't get out of bed that's what.

"You like to leave."

Don Draper can't stay, won't stay. He does not know who he is, and has no rudder. When Sylvia says this to him one morning in bed, she wants to be cute, playful. Things are still fun, and he's only leaving for work, but of course it is fraught with implication. He will leave, whether he likes it or not. It's not a choice, and this isn't *LOST*. He doesn't have choices, he is what he is, even if he doesn't know what that is. I want to leave at times too, and not in an *I want to desert my family sort of way*, more like, *I need to take a work trip sort of way*, because it's a lot, parenting, being on, and responsive, all the time, from the second I walk through the door until I leave again. And sometimes because of that I just want to crumble in the hall by the front door before I even walk in. Something Don does as the closing credits roll, and "Just a Gigolo" plays, albeit not the David Lee Roth opus, because this is *Mad Men* and not *LOST*, so sadly no one is time traveling.

"I don't know what we're doing."

How could Sylvia know what she and Don are doing? Don who said he and Megan were drifting apart, yet still somehow got her pregnant. Don who gives her money after sex and who could maybe want more, though we know better, as does Sylvia. Things will end poorly, they have to. This is *Mad Men*, not *Two and a Half Men*. And herein lies the rub: you never quite feel like you know what you're doing when it comes to parenting, and jokes aside about the lack of training manuals, you don't know. You listen, you guide, you try to stay engaged and be empathic. But at the end of the day as you lie in bed with your partner or the child themselves, you don't know shit, and you can't do anything to quite shake that feeling. The only thing you can truly do is decide whether you're in or you're out, and if you're in, you need to buckle-up.

"I've never said no to you."
Before Trudy slams the door on Pete, she reminds him that she has never said no to him, not about his apartment in the city, nor his mistresses, to which Pete replies that they left the city for her, and are now trapped in the suburbs, aren't they? Which points to one of the great conundrums of communications of any kind—we know what we know when we say it, and we know what we know when we hear it—it's just that what we hear, and how we are heard has more to do with who we are than what was said. Pete will always feel put upon. It's who he is, and who he will be, which again is *Mad Men* at its most fundamental. People don't change, they can't. They just change houses or jobs, and possibly grow sideburns. Our children change. It takes a while to know anything about that, but what we do know, is that they

think we say no all the time, and they are right, we do, sometimes blatantly, and sometimes with our body language. At times, this is because we think we are making good choices for them, less candy for example, and other times it is selfish, we cannot bear to watch *Caillou* even one more time. The hardest thing is fighting that. We're so tired, and we just want things to be easier, which is a tension all in itself. Pete and Trudy want things to be easier as well, it's just that like our children, they have their own interpretations of what that means.

"Well it can't be that bad when you're doing something you love."

If you love what you're doing it can never be bad, right? Which is another *Mad Men* trope that they circle back to again and again. Yes, we are selling baked beans or dreams, cigarettes even, but we love the thrill of doing so, the chase, the creativity, the energy of getting it right, and that makes all of our other behaviors and regrets okay. It has to. Aren't we all just seeking to love something, anything? Of course we are. So it is with parenting as well. It's terrible, painful, endlessly frustrating, and scary, but there is so much love involved so much of the time, we would probably burst if not for the basic physics that govern the world. And this is why we keep going, and ignore our own regrets. When it's right, there's nothing like it. Not unlike *Mad Men* itself.

The Lion King

When my nephew was five, and before I had children of my own, I took him to see *The Emperor's Last Groove*, and then out to Haagen-Dazs for ice cream.

"What did you think of the movie?" I said.

"What did I think?" he said. "I think that this was the best day of my life."

Which was very cute, but would have been much cuter, if he hadn't clearly been planning a bait and switch all along.

"Is your dad dead?" he asked suddenly, no lead-in, no change in expression.

I wasn't sure what to say. No one had prepped me for this. He wasn't even my child. What would his parents want me to say?

I did the best I could.

"He is, sweetie," I said.

"Is he in New York City?" he asked.

"You know, he could be," I said, "I think he'd really like to think so."

He smiled. I smiled. The trap was set.

"Is my dad going to die too?" he asked.

Fuck.

"He is baby, but not for a very long time," I said, because that's what I had heard you are supposed to say.

He didn't respond to this, which may be an apt response.

Fast forward ten years, Noah is five and we are watching *The Lion King*. As the Mufasa death scene approaches, Noah shows no sign of concern, no nothing actually, no questions, no movement, just pure engrossment.

Then moments before Mufasa's death, Noah says, "Fast forward, please."

"Why?" I ask. "And do you want to talk about it?"

"I don't like that scene," Noah responds, "and you know Mufasa doesn't die anyway."

He doesn't? Mufasa has always seemed pretty dead to me following that scene. Like dead, dead, as it were.

"Really," I say, "he's not dead? I thought he was."

"No," Noah says, "he's not, because he's in the clouds later, and that's not dead is it?"

Damn, I had to initiate this?

"Well," I say, "some people would say that the dead are always with us in some way, in our hearts, and memories, and so Mufasa is always with Simba in that fashion."

Not a bad answer, whether or not I believe it.

"So, Dada Mike, he's always with us too?" Noah said.

And there it is.

He is not. Not to me. Do I think about my dad? Yes. Is he in my heart? Yes. Do I think he's out in the clouds and in ponds and looking for chances to speak with me and encourage me to reach my full potential? No. Sorry. I don't

believe that. I also resent it when other people tell me he is always with me in some form or another, which brings me to the movie *Frequency*.

In *Frequency*, Dennis Quaid plays a fireman with a ham radio who dies in a factory fire. Jim Caviezel, (yes, that one, Jesus, Son of God) plays his son who grows up to be a drunken, bitter cop who one night turns on the old ham radio and re-connects with his father at a point some time before his actual death, ultimately changing the course of history and bringing his dad into the present. To which I, and the creators of *LOST*, say bullshit.

Because when your dad dies, you don't get him back. He doesn't get to meet your sons or give you advice and he certainly doesn't show up in the clouds or on old ham radios. He's just dead and you have to figure out how to cope with that.

None of which I share with Noah, because that arguably seems like bad parenting to me.

Instead I say to him, "Yes, baby, my dad is in the clouds," leaving any deeper conversations about death and the Circle of Life for some other, and more appropriate, time.

You might ask of course what that appropriate time is, and I will tell you that I still don't know, and I don't know how to figure that out.

I never even thought about death until my dad died, I became a father, and I began wondering if I would outlive him. The conversation usually goes like this:

"He lived until fifty-nine," I say to myself, "that's it, and that's only fourteen years from now. That's plenty of time to write, which is good, because there are a lot of things I want to write about."

"Cool, but what about the boys?" I respond.

"Fuck," I say.

"Right, I mean do the math bro," I reply.

"I don't want to do the math," I say, "I don't even like math."

But that's just one of the many ways thinking about death starts messing with you. It makes you think about all kinds of things you would rather ignore.

"It's cool," I say to myself, "I'll do the math. Myles is eleven. Noah is seven. Which means, that if I only make it to 59 they will be 25 and 21 respectively, and yes, they will be young men, and yes, I will get to see them through high school, and maybe, at least one of them through college. But what about weddings and grandchildren? That's not clear, and I'm sorry about that."

"And what about the fact that they could be fatherless like me?" I reply. "What does that mean, and how do you even begin to calculate the impact of that?"

"I'm not clear about that either," I say, "and I'm definitely sorry about that."

The fact is, being an uncle might occasionally be tough, but being a father has skewed and fucked everything. The boys are now my filter, and when I'm happy, or sad, selfish or benevolent, all you have to ask is what role they played in that feeling, what the affect is on them, or what any of that means in terms of being the kind of father I want to be, even if I cannot define what that is much of the time.

Not that I would change any of this or go back to the time before I was a father. If I did, who else would kick me in the balls and pretend to be Beast from X-Men? Or parade around the apartment naked and shaking their ass? And who else would I watch grow-up before me and then someday leave us, only to have these same kinds of fears themselves, as they too grow-old, improbably mind you, and awesome?

Ultimately, my plan these days is not to die at 59, or even die at all if I can swing it, and so any role you, the reader, can play in accomplishing this would be great. Now, what might that role be? I'm not sure about that either, but buying more of my books can't hurt. Think about it, and then go do the right thing, thanks.

The Penis Stories

When our older son was born, and we will call him Zach to protect the innocent, he had a skin tag on his fore-skin. Skin tags are those small, extra, mutant pieces of skin that suddenly appear on your body one day, unannounced and unwelcomed. You may have had one on your face or chest. You may have ignored it or had it removed. You may have even brushed against it on occasion causing it to bleed. They are annoying, but for the most part they are no big deal.

I once had one burned off of my face in a deserted building under the train tracks on Wabash that clearly doubled as a clandestine mob doctor's office. The skin tag is still gone, however, and I'm still here, so no harm, no foul as far as I can see.

This one though was on Zach's penis. I wanted to ignore it, but I couldn't. It was his penis, and I was fixated on it. I suppose this might raise some questions about dads and penises, or at least this dad and penises, but at the time we were planning Zach's bris. A bris is a Jewish ritual akin to clipping the top off of a fine Cuban cigar, but with religious implications. Something to do with a temple and oil I believe.

I had become obsessed with the possibility that the mohel, the person who performs the bris, was going to accidentally get caught on the skin tag, slip, and cut too deeply, hence changing any ideas we had about Zach's gender and upbringing.

Now, before we go any further, I understand that penises have little to do with a person's understanding of their own gender, that penises may even be some kind of social construct, but I'm not sure I got that then, not when this little creature that had been entrusted to us was about to receive a procedure I hadn't remotely begun to wrap my brain around.

I can now also appreciate that I might have been over thinking this, but it was all so new, and when there is so much unknown flying around, it's much easier to focus on concrete things like skin tags, even when they are on a baby's penis.

When the mohel came to meet us a few days before the bris for a sort of informational interview, he asked us whether we had any questions.

"Do you see this skin tag?" I asked, forcibly directing him to look at Zach's penis. "Is that going to be a problem?"

"No, not at all," he said.

"Are you sure?" I said.

"Very much so," he said, "I've performed thousands of these."

"But have you ever seen a skin tag like that one?" I asked, a perverse sort of reverse pride emerging.

"Do you have any questions about the ceremony it-self?" he asked, ignoring me.

"No," I said, chastened, but still obsessing.

The mohel was right. There were no problems with the circumcision. Well, not exactly. What I should I say is that there were no physical problems, but there were psychic ones, the problems were mine though, and not those of Zach, or later, his younger brother Slater.

The problem was that first Zach's penis and then Slater's, looked fairly large to me at birth, large enough anyway, and this had made me happy, but what they don't tell you about circumcisions, is that when the hood is gone, much of the size goes with it, and seeing this made me sad.

I have male friends who have told me that they didn't want to be fathers to boys, that they felt their fathers were not good role models, and so what could they possibly have to offer their own sons? These are intelligent, caring men, who are good husbands and will be great dads, and I never understood where they were coming from. I know I am going to do everything I can to be a good father by modeling confidence even when I'm lacking it, providing positive reinforcement, and looking to build their self-esteem in a healthy manner. I also know I will fail them as a man in some fashion. Hopefully Debbie, a coach, a teacher, a girlfriend, or boyfriend, will fill-in for my glaring limitations, but there is no question in my mind that a larger penis would help ameliorate these problems from the start.

This was re-affirmed for me one afternoon when I took Zach into the bathroom and we were joined by one his friends and his dad. Let's call the friend Screech. Screech swaggered up to the urinal like he owned the place, and I soon knew why. He was hung like a horse, a small horse maybe, but even adults were looking at him enviously. Was he circumcised? Not at all, but was he happy, and confident, yes, and why shouldn't he be?

He should, and speaking of happy, I should mention here, that both Zach and Slater had colic as babies, with Zach's colic reaching near epic proportions. Colic is commonly defined as intensive crying for three or more hours a stretch three days a week. Zach often cried fifteen to twenty hours a day, every day, for nine weeks. Slater was a slight improvement. He didn't start screaming until early afternoon, but would regularly continue after that until midnight. This lasted for twelve weeks.

Doctors don't really know what causes colic, or how to treat it. Just that it eventually ends on its own, disappearing as quickly and mysteriously as it sets in. In spite of this, there are still an endless series of suggestions about how best to soothe such babies. You can take them for a drive, swaddle them, run the vacuum cleaner, purchase a swing with an uterine swoosh as we did; or maybe set them on top of a dryer. None of these things worked for us though. And we tried everything. Well, almost everything.

We read somewhere on the internet, possibly on www.nauseatingoldwivestales.com, that in Chinese culture mothers will masturbate their colic-y male new-borns to calm them. A baby happy ending if you will. We were desperate, but not that desperate. Still, I wondered whether this was true or urban myth. I also wondered whether if true, if this was a current practice or something from the distant past, and whether there was any real research that proved it worked regardless, as opposed to moving, yet anecdotal testimonies from celebrities like Jessica Simpson? I was too scared to Google it any further, because who needs to end up like Pete Townshend? Not this guy, as Noah, I mean Slater, might say. I also considered asking one of my many Chinese friends if it was true, but I really wasn't sure how to go about it.

"So," I considered saying, "your baby has colic right, and you're Chinese, do you masturbate him, you know, so you can soothe him? And if so, does it help?"

This seemed culturally insensitive to me, however, when said out loud, and I haven't pursued it any further. I still wonder though, even if at this point it is for academic reasons.

And speaking of academics, one day, Zach and I were walking to school and discussing current events, such as whether or not we thought Lindsay Lohan's current stay in rehabilitation would be beneficial for her health and career. Zach loves Lohan's work in the remake of the *Parent Trap*, and I love her because she is young and skanky, and I am old and have been married to the same person for many years.

"I want to kiss your penis," Zach said suddenly with a big smile on his face.

I admired his candor and his correct usage of penis, but this was somewhat alarming, especially since we were in public, and the homeless lady by Jewel was now staring at us more than usual. Further, what had prompted this? Did he know it would freak me out? Or was that giving him too much credit? Was it some desire to merge with me in some way? And if so, what does that mean exactly, because *Parent* magazine throws that phrase around like I should already know?

"Hey buddy," I said to Zach, "do you want to tell me why you just said that?"

"No," he said still smiling.

"Are you sure?" I asked.

"Yes," he said.

"Okay, but why would you say that?" I said a little more desperately, now kind of repeating myself since I didn't know what else to say.

"No reason. Because I want to," he said.

"You know," I said, "if you have to say that, please only do so at home, not in public, and never in school. Okay? Daddy does not want to go to jail."

"Okay," he said.

Having fixed that, I dropped Zach off at school and went to work. When I got home I asked the babysitter what she had done with the boys after Zach was done with school.

"We visited Screech and Kelly," she said.

Kelly is Screech's sister.

"And while we were there," she continued, "I heard Kelly say, 'we can't see mommy's vagina because there's so much hair.'"

"Lovely," I said, "though kind of weird, right?"

"Yes," she said, "but then Zach said to her, I kiss my dad's penis."

The babysitter smiled. She didn't say anything else.

"I will talk to him," I said.

I sat down with Zach after school and I explained again, that he shouldn't say that in public, and he agreed, again, that comments about said body part and what he does with them are better left for private, if said at all. I in turn agreed to buy him a pony, though I made no promises regarding how well hung said pony might be.

Race Matters

Myles was always adamant. He is adamant about everything, but this maybe more so.

He would not dash.

Not ever.

No way.

The office has a run. It's a fundraiser. There is a 5k, a 10k, and a walk. There are mascots—the Berenstain Bears and Benny the Bull—family activities, involving things like water balloons and bean bags.

There is also a kids' dash.

But he won't dash, and I cannot let it go, and so every year the conversation goes something like this:

"Yo, this is the year you are going to run the dash, right? Yes. Sweet, you are."

"No, never. Not this year, not ever, you know that," he says.

"It's not going to be windy," I say, "I totally checked that already."

He doesn't like the wind. Not that I actually checked whether it will be windy. The race is weeks away, and who's to say what the weather will bring.

And yes, please note I have just lied to him. Parents do that a lot. I could defend it as a necessary means for getting through the day. I could also acknowledge that it is very poor modeling. Then again, if we're going to get into modeling, and poor examples thereof, we will be here forever.

"That's not it," he says.

"The mascots will leave you alone," I say. "Promise. I know a guy who knows a guy and arrangements have been made."

He doesn't dig mascots either. I don't totally get it myself but that doesn't mean I can't also acknowledge how weird a sweaty, faux fur covered, beast with an enormous head and unmoving eyes might be to a child.

"No, that's not it either," he says turning away.

"What is it then?" I ask. "What? Why? What?"

"Nothing, I don't want to do it," he says. "Not even for you."

"Do you want a pony?" I ask. "Maybe we could get a spot for him or her in the parking garage?"

"No."

No is no with him, which will certainly be an admirable trait when I'm finished raising him. So that's done, again, and no I don't know exactly why this is, and why he won't run.

"Why do you think he won't dash?" I ask myself.

"It has something do with anxiety, and control, and pressure," I respond, "and maybe the fact that I am such a prick and that I want it so much, which of course can only bring more stress.

"But I don't know for sure, so I tell myself I don't care."

"Just like you don't care about soccer, T-ball, basketball, golf, or judo?" I ask myself.

"Yes, if he doesn't want to do sports and he prefers the theater, it's fine, theater is cool. More than cool," I say. "I like theater and improv too. So it's cool, really. Sports, running, whatever, that can be my thing, and my thing alone."

"So, it's totally fine," I say, "no problem, great."

"Sure, now, does that mean that I never lie to myself when it comes to parenting?" I respond. "And let's be clear, I have already established the fact that I lie to my children. This is about whether I ever lie to myself about my children, the act of parenting them, and whatever might come in between."

"Yes, okay," I say, "go with that."

"For the record," I say, "when Debbie first got pregnant, I also said I didn't care about whether he was boy or a girl as long as he was healthy. But was that true? Maybe, but when he came out, all slippery, covered with muck, upside down, and spewing his crazy hair, only to finally flip over and reveal his penis, was I happy to see it, or more accurately, happier than I may have been otherwise?"

"Were you?" I ask.

"Fuck, yes," I say. "And what about when he had colic, and I said I didn't even care if he worked at AM/PM when he was an adult as long as he stopped crying all the time. Was I lying then?"

"I think I know the answer to that," I say.

"Again, yes, of course I was," I say. "Are you kidding? He's going to make cool documentaries that they will rave about at South by Southwest. Dance with the Joffrey Ballet. Win a Nobel Peace Prize for his work in war-torn countries. Become the first Jewish president, a Supreme Court Justice, the next Pope or Dalai Lama, definitely, possibly, who knows."

"So, when you bring up the dash every year," I say, "that doesn't mean anything either, right?"

"No it doesn't, not at all," I say. "As I said, it's cool, totally."

And that conversation is over, except that I'm a fucking liar, and I am dying for him to run that fucking dash.

So, maybe the question then, is what the fuck is wrong with me?

Let's break it down.

There are a lot of things about me that suck—rage, avoidance, indecisiveness, confusion, anxiety—and you don't have to take my word for it either, just ask my children, wife, therapist, mom, or co-workers. But running helps me manage these things, and so maybe what this is about is the great power and freedom I have found in running, which I want to believe that if he opened himself to the possibility of he could find too.

Of course, we can't make people do the things we think will be helpful, even our kids. We can suggest, and we can cajole, but at some point we need to step back, which sucks, even if it's right.

Ultimately though, I wonder if it's something much simpler than documentaries, and freedom. I want him to feel more normal, and not later, being normal later will be of no benefit to him. But now, as a kid, and a little boy who goes to public school and gets teased because he isn't into sports. Maybe running the dash, something everyone else seems to be comfortable with, would help him get by, and help him see that other activities deemed "normal," like playing soccer before school, aren't so bad.

To be clear, I'm not an advocate of normal as better, even when it's easier, but since he can't quite embrace the state of being not normal yet either, and we can't seem to help him do so, wouldn't it be easier for him at this point in his life?

You might say, life isn't easy and everyone has to learn that, but why can't we put that off as long as possible? What's the rush for him to learn this?

"You don't know what it's like being me," Myles tells me.

I couldn't embrace being not normal myself—the comic book collecting, not being into sports, and bad lunches—so I used to think that I knew what he was going through, that we could connect, but I was wrong, and he was right.

When people teased me I punched them and they stopped, and later I just ran from it, literally, but he won't do any of that, which I admire. He's better than me.

Which leaves us where?

It leaves us here, at the starting line, sort of. I'll explain.

There is also Noah, and he runs the dash the first year he can. He cries. But he does it. His balloon bracelet in place and baggy sweat pants pooling around his ankles. It's breathtaking, and though Myles shows no reaction to Noah running, when he's done, I wonder if Myles will have to succumb to peer pressure and dash as well.

But he doesn't.

Could using that have been a more effective means for pressuring him into running? Not really, but I could have tried.

"Yo, did you see that, Noah just ripped it up, tears and all," I might have said, "what do you say, is this your year too?"

He would not have responded.

"I'm just saying, that was pretty cool, right?" I might have said next, "and not so scary looking, was it? No one got knocked over, everyone had fun. It could be fun, couldn't it?"

He would continue not to respond.

"Anyway, it's cool, whatever you want," I would finally say.

I didn't do that though, because he's not willing to succumb to something like that. And there's something sort of beautiful in that too, and again, something that will serve him well later. It's just that it's always later.

You might ask here, if Noah's interest in the dash impacts my feelings about Myles lack of interest? It does, it makes me love Myles more fiercely, and it only solidifies my belief that it will all work out, if not now, later, and that it, this, life, will be fine.

Which I imagine could be another conversation.

"It's cool, if you don't want to dash, you have your own mind, and you're on your own path, and I love that," I could say.

But I don't. Even positivity can feel like a pressure, and the whole event is so fraught with tension because of my needs that I just back off.

Which might raise another question, how do I feel then, when Myles decides to finally dash the following year, walks up to the starting line, and just like the mascots and the wind, the dogs, and all of those things that once seemed so impossible to overcome, he is now done not dashing as well, just like that.

Because there he is, and he is off, his legs all askew, but strong, his arms pumping, his expression determined, powerful, and magnificent.

What do I say then? Maybe the better question is what did he say to me?

"You happy?" he asks after he is done.

"Yeah," I say. "What prompted that?"

"Nothing," he says.

And then he walks away.

He has done it his way, and when he was ready to do it. Not when I was ready for him to do it, which is sometimes sooner, usually later, but always his way, regardless.

You Throw Your Life in My Face

Debbie and I lived in New York City together and never talked about having children. Then we decided to move to Chicago and still didn't talk about it. We didn't know Chicago: we had never been there. We went to Burton Place on Burton and Wells because we saw they were showing that night's Knicks-Bulls play-off game.

We drank with some guys we did not know, and Scottie Pippen refused to enter the game as a decoy. We asked the guys where ex-New Yorkers who didn't have a car should live and they sketched out the corner of Goethe and Dearborn on a used cocktail napkin.

"There is a coffee shop right there," they said, "the Red line and Jewel are around the corner. There are buses. It's perfect."

"Okay," we said.

The next day we went to Relcon, an apartment finding service, and we showed the young woman there our cocktail napkin.

"We want to live here," we said.

"Okay," she said.

And after that we got an apartment above The 3rd Coast Coffee Shop.

Sometimes you pick a place, and sometimes it picks you. I used to be embarrassed to live in a neighborhood known as the Gold Coast. I was even embarrassed that our apartment was clean and spacious and big and somehow cheaper than the seedy studio we lived-in in New York City.

But there we were, and we still didn't talk about children, or how we might someday raise them in a neighborhood we grew to love. And here we are so many years later, raising children in the Gold Coast having only moved once and only across the street at that.

We may leave the neighborhood eventually, but it will always be the kids' first neighborhood no matter how where we end-up or how much it continues to change while we are still here.

I suppose this is a love letter to a neighborhood that seems so different to me than when we first moved here. Or it may just be a series of memories about a neighborhood in transition that I want to be sure that I share with my children. It may even be both. Either way, here we go.

It's 6:00am. It's still dark, and the sun is just coming up, its long purple tendrils beginning to spread across the neighborhood. I'm heading out for a run and Debbie is still asleep. I walk out of the apartment and then, realizing I left my keys behind head back in. As I rummage around for the keys on the telephone table I sense someone standing behind me in our apartment and I turn around.

It's one of our neighbors, someone we rarely ever see. He looks disoriented. Pale. I've never really looked at him up close before. His skin is mottled and pockmarked, his hair thin and wispy. This scene is definitely odd, but he doesn't seem especially threatening, just out of it in some way.

"Hey man, what's up?" I say.

He purses his lips, trying to form words that get lost somewhere in his mouth before they can emerge. I stare at him wondering what my next move should be.

"Your—your, door was open," he says stammering. "I came in to close it, because that's not safe."

"No, no, it's not." I say, "Thank you so much. I'm here though, and I'm going back out, so it's cool, ok?"

"Yeah sure," he says, before turning around and wandering off into the morning.

We have now lived in the neighborhood for nearly twenty years, and while my sense of the neighborhood may exist mostly in my head, the slow death of any neighborhood deserves to be recognized, especially when that death arguably represents not only something larger going on in this city we all love, loathe, celebrate, and care about so much, but something the boys will never quite be able to experience.

To begin, a less-than-scientific look at some of the places the neighborhood has lost including both The Esquire and Village movie theaters. For years The Village employed a hulking, bearded, red-haired, near-mute Viking ticket taker whom I prayed would never sit next to me when I had the theater to myself. And he never did. On the other hand, it was at The Village where we watched a guy jerk off during *Leaving Las Vegas*. It was kind of untoward certainly, but as no one ever seems to jerk off at the AMC 21 East, I am left with a certain sense of nostalgia.

The Hotsy-Totsy is also gone. And while I recognize that according to the blog *What White People Like*, I am supposed to like dive bars, it was the last great dive bar in the neighborhood, and we had many late night drinks at its moist, crusty tables. It is now a CVS, one of two in the neighborhood, and it's not just that we can't drink there anymore on the nights we occasionally still stumble home, but the kids will never have the chance to do so either.

Not that I'm encouraging them to drink, but if they happen to, the Hotsy-Totsy was certainly a far better option than the Hangge-Uppe or Mother's will ever be.

The pizza joint Ranalli's is gone as well, pushed out of its old, decrepit brownstone at the corner of Dearborn and Elm. My bachelor party was held in the private room upstairs and it was there that we had the opportunity to make the acquaintance of one Melanie Melons. She did not join us to talk neighborhoods or children, but she did school us on the proper proportion of whipped cream to bare breast.

Late one morning, Debbie and I are walking north

up Dearborn. It is several years after my first encounter with the neighbor. It turns that he is a musician. He plays at night, and the morning I first met him he was just getting home from a gig. He's also an alcoholic. We see him in front of Edwardo's, sitting in the gutter, trying to regain his balance, one hand on the curb, one reaching for heights far beyond his limited range of motion. He can't get up and he's staring at us, or through us, pleading with someone, maybe us, maybe the voices in his head, to help him. He falls down one more time, now lying in the street, no chance of getting up. We walk by him, eyes straight ahead, the least caring thing we've ever done.

Later, of course, we will have to explain things like why people drunkenly sit in gutters to Myles and Noah, but we didn't have to yet, it was still just the two of us then.

Millionaire Lee Migilin was murdered over on Astor by serial killer Andrew Cunanan, who stopped to shave before heading off to Miami to kill Gianni Versace. On Schiller, a super murdered his whole family in a townhouse where he worked and then neatly lined them up in the basement so they could rest peacefully.

There haven't been too many killings lately, nothing like these anyway, murders that spoke somehow to an older, more romantic and grizzled Chicago which doesn't seem to exist anymore. Now it's guns and beefs and neighborhood guys settling fights with bullets.

Still before all that, or at least before there seemed to be so many more guns and shootings, we did once kind of witness a murder on the northeast corner of Goethe and Dearborn.

At the time we still lived up above The 3rd Coast, the home of the greatest coronation chicken salad you've ever had. The apartment faced north and overlooked the courtyard of the now long-closed Three Arts Club. During the summer we watched the weddings being held there from our window and then danced along with the guests during the receptions.

With a little work we could also look east out of those windows and initially like many apartments in the neighborhood we could see a sliver of lake if we looked at just the right angle. Our view was unimpeded, because we faced a parking lot, but this changed over time as the first of what was to become one of many new high rises in the neighborhood was being built. We watched it go up floor by floor as we simultaneously watched our view disappear.

One hot summer night we lay in bed, the windows wide-open following a brownout. It was quiet, except for the occasional passing car or person returning home from the bars on Division. As we tried to stay cool, the screams started, emanating from the new building still being constructed across the street. It was a woman and she was in great distress.

"Stop, no, stop, you're going to kill me!" she screamed.

Debbie and I looked at each other silently, frozen in place. Someone else would deal with this, right? Someone else would make the call. The screaming continued.

"Nooooooooooooooooooo!"

We stared out the window, not seeing a thing.

"Call the police," Debbie said. "Please, call."

It was the right thing to do, but I was scared. I dialed 9-1-1.

"Someone is being attacked, a woman, at the northeast corner of Goethe and Dearborn," I said. "It's coming from the new building. Please hurry."

We sat by the window waiting, listening to the endless screams, and within ninety seconds, two, three, four, then five police cars pulled up to the building. A police officer got out carrying a bullhorn.

"Come out with your hands above your head or we're coming in," he shouted.

The screaming stopped. It was silent. Then people started moving around. There was some commotion. We couldn't tell who was who or what was happening. The cop picked up the bull horn again.

"You've got to be fucking kidding me!" he said, exasperated. "You're filming a fucking movie? All of you get the fuck out here now."

Myles and Noah love this story. It's scary, but safe, and kids like that, the sense that they can control their fears. What they cannot control any more than we can is the incessant change overtaking the neighborhood, and so we keep reminding them of what the neighborhood looked like when they were little, or before they were born, somehow hoping they will absorb all the things that were so appealing to us.

There was a time when there wasn't an upscale, fully appointed, studio, one, two, or three-bedroom, three and a half bathroom, concierge services available, duplex, 24-hour doorman, high-end appliances, great view, gold-plated, marble countertops, luxurious, world-class views, central air, exercise room, exclusive, magnificent, spectacular, the sky is bluer, people friendlier, grass greener, girls prettier, sex is better, can't be beat, private, and unique, fully ubiquitous high rise on every corner.

Back then, for example, there was Gold Coast Video at Dearborn and Division, a great video store specializing in independent movies and gay porn. It was swallowed up along with the Ranalli's to make room for another of the not-to-be-missed new buildings.

Don and Chad managed Gold Coast Video. Don was short, aged, bespectacled, hoodie-wearing, and bald, though not by choice. And Chad was young, buff, bespectacled, hoodie-wearing, and bald, as a fashion statement. Don and Chad loved movies, all movies, they held an Oscar night contest, had two-for-one rental Wednesdays, and endlessly recommended obscure movies they thought we would love.

Debbie and I regularly stopped by the store just to argue about new movies, who had seen them first, what we liked, didn't like, and what other movies they reminded us of.

After Debbie and I saw the glorious wreck *Eyes Wide Shut*, a movie we had all been talking about for at least a year, we went to the store to see what Don thought.

"What do I think?" he said. "I think I don't care who my partner sleeps with as long as he loves me the best."

Myles and Noah will never meet Don or Chad, which seems impossible to us. We never saw them outside of the store, and yet there was a time where they felt like family. That was a long time ago though, when we were still young. There were no children, and everything in the neighborhood still felt so new.

There was also a Barbara's Bookstore in the neighborhood then over on Wells that had a children's section they would have loved. It's a bank now.

I saw Art Spiegelman there and sat in awe the whole time he spoke. When I saw Scott Heim the author of *Mysterious Skin* read, he made me want to do readings myself one day because of his absolute sense of calm and mastery. Hearing Don DeGrazia read *American Skin* at Barbara's convinced me I should try and be a novelist because it seemed like the kind of book I might be able to write if the novel gods ever decided to smile on me.

And then there was Lynda Barry, known best for her comics, but also the author of *Cruddy*, one of my favorite novels of that year or any year. I almost never ask writers questions at readings, but she was an exception. I had just really started writing when I saw her, but I had the sense that she could provide me with some insights about how to improve what I was trying to do.

"How do you write such funny comics one day," I asked, "and then write something so dark like *Cruddy* the next? Do you plan something like that?"

"No," she said, "I just write what I'm feeling that day."

And now so do I. The boys don't know me in any other way. It doesn't matter to them that I couldn't get started once, and that I only began writing when I moved into the neighborhood. But it matters to me. The neighborhood has always possessed a sort of magic, and I can only hope that some of that magic rubs off on them.

I'm walking north up State Street towards Division with Myles, then three and a half, and we have just left the neighborhood Barnes & Noble. They don't host readings, or have "staff recommended" books with little descriptions like Barbara's did, but they have books, and Myles loves books, and it's walking distance so we do what we can.

It's Myles' neighborhood now as well, and soon enough Noah will be born and it will become his too. And no, they will never go to Gold Coast Video to rent porn with us or Ranalli's for pizza. Nor will they have breakfast at Monday's, the greasy diner we once frequented at State and Division, or stumble some day in to the Hotsy-Totsy. But they have Five Faces for hot dogs and Gouty playground. They love The Third Coast and they don't really know what's been lost, despite how much we talk about it.

But at this point, there is no Noah yet, just Myles, and we're focused on lunch and maybe watching Barney. The sun is out, and it's been a good day. As we start to cross Elm, the people in front of us merge and unmerge and the neighbor suddenly appears, standing in the middle of the sidewalk, facing south, facing us. I haven't seen him since Debbie and I saw him collapse in the gutter now several years before. He's unsteady on his feet and wildly flailing his arms. I take Myles' hand and see whether we can cross the street. The neighbor looks right at us and then he points his finger at me and starts to shout.

"You mock me like this!" he shouts. "You throw your life in my face!"

He looks stricken. Can he possibly remember who I am? And if he does, does he resent me for becoming a parent, deserting him, and changing with the neighborhood, even as he remains stuck in the neighborhood as it once was? Have I betrayed him in some way?

I pull on Myles' wrist and drag him east across the street.

As I look back, the neighbor is flailing his arms again, no longer talking. People pass by him, eyes down, horrified, and saddened. The sun is slicing between the buildings, where it can, enveloping him in a soft, hazy, afternoon glow. He's illuminated now, and fixed in time, his arms raised high above him. The neighbor is silently raging at the heavens, and looking for answers that no one down here can provide him with.

No Avoiding That

It is so late and my brain is as purple and full of fury as Myles' tiny face. He is four weeks old and he has been crying all day, every day, for three weeks.

He doesn't nap. He doesn't even doze off, except for the rare, and brief, moments when he falls asleep on our chests as we are sitting on the couch and we are able to avoid movement of any kind, including breathing, blinking, and involuntary muscle spasms.

Otherwise, he is awake and crying, at times passing out from his efforts, which requires us to splash water on his face to wake him.

He sleeps four to five hours straight per night, which is nice, but not usually any more than that.

I can tell you now that this will be over by nine weeks, just like that, like magic. One day he will be crying all-day, and the next he won't.

But that's still five weeks away from this moment. Tonight it is he and I alone in the living room, the lights off, the occasional car passing by below.

He is lying on his boppy pillow across from me on the ottoman as I stay sitting and motionless in our big ass chair.

Nothing will soothe him and I am exhausted. I should wake Debbie, but I feel like I am on my own, and this is my cross to bear.

I stare at him and I try to remind myself that he is suffering.

As he continues crying though, that feeling of empathy passes and hardens into something else, something angry and frustrated and full of confusion about what he needs.

I picture lifting him by his miniature shoulders, shaking him, and yelling, "What do you want?"

I tell myself not to move, not even one inch, not a muscle, nothing. *Just breathe* I think. *Ride the wave of tears and anger, and the moment will pass.*

And it does, finally, and at some point we are both able to sleep.

Still, I wanted to grab him, shake him, and scream, and there's no avoiding that. I do not recall ever feeling that kind of rage towards an adult. Of course, there's no adult I can't walk away from. Myles is different though, we are bound together and there's no walking away from him, not ever.

Sometimes, however, there is no turning away either. And what I should do then? How should I make sense about what is discipline and what is violence, even if it's only being experienced in my head? And what should that discipline look like? Because there's the rub, things aren't always happening in my head, sometimes they do get more physical.

One morning, and honestly it could be any morning in terms of the frenzy, but I am thinking of this one morning in particular. We are trying to get out of the house, and there are school bags to pack and teeth to brush, both mine and the boys' and I need to put on work clothes, and Myles and Noah need hats, and lunches need to be made, and there are the socks that do not fit, no matter how hard I try to make it so, and I am flying around the house, and I want to believe that they may soon settle-down.

But Noah is crying and will not stop, not ever maybe, and there is the stress of knowing that I cannot make it to work on time, not with the two of them at different schools, not with Debbie already out of the house, and the crying, hats, socks, teeth, all of that piling-up on top of each other.

And then suddenly, in the midst of all this, I start to believe that I may really get out of the house, because suddenly they are ready, and why can't I be too? I can, and so I leave them up front by the door and I run into the kitchen.

The tears get louder. Why is that happening? It's possible that that they are magnified by the foyer and its funky acoustics, but then there is wailing, and I run back to the foyer, and Myles is standing by the doors that open into the hall leading to our rooms, holding them shut so that that Noah cannot step into the front of the house.

Hence the tears and the wailing and the increased frenzy that I just want so badly to go away. I look at Myles.

He's smiling and entirely pleased with what he's done.

This is a great time to breathe, count to ten, something, instead, my brain briefly explodes, and all I can see and hear, is the crying, the heat, the rushing around and the frenzy, so much fucking frenzy.

As the sweat starts to pool on my upper lip and slither along my brow, and as the words in my head start to morph into something that sounds a lot like the white noise that passes for conversation among the adults in *Peanuts*, things don't exactly blur together, but they do start to go a little dark.

Which is not to say I cannot tell what is happening, I am watching it happen, but I am not in control, not really, maybe not even close.

I see what I am doing and I understand that I am grasping the collar of Myles' coat, that I am lifting him off of the ground, and moving him away from the doors, which I now open as he stands there gape-mouthed, caught somewhere between bemusement and shock.

Noah stands in front of me in the hall red-faced and perspiring, screaming and shaking, a physical manifestation of the emotions pin-balling around my frenzied brain.

And it is here, now, that this question of discipline and what it might look like starts to re-appear in my tired brain. Though if it wasn't that moment exactly, it was certainly later that day as I was walking home from school with the boys and I heard Myles say to one of his friends, "My dad tried to strangle me this morning."

Which I would argue is not true, not really, but that doesn't change the fact that I can so easily be moved to rage, even as the idea of corporal punishment has never felt like an option to me.

I was not hit as a child, and I do not believe in hitting children. No slaps, no brushes, or spanks, but this does not change the fact that I was moved to act in a physical way, or that I still believe that raising children requires discipline, and that there must be consequences when they do not manage their crueler, and yes, more annoying impulses.

Still, if these consequences do not involve spanking, they better involve something. Something they can learn from and I can try to master so that I do not lose my shit in some way that everyone ends up regretting.

I could pause here for a moment and reflect on the fact that there was no discipline in my house growing-up, that there was an element of needing to make do, that there was love, always, and endlessly, but we had to figure things out for ourselves, which when coupled with my parents just not being around as much as my wife and I are, ultimately required less of a need for discipline in the first place. All of which may say something about how Debbie and I parent, or about who I am and what I still need to fix. Though more likely it's both.

Which I get, but for now, let me say this, if there is to be frenzy, and there will be, there has to be, I'm glad we have the time-out, because that can be a beautiful thing. I don't have to lay my hands on the boys, though if needed it can be brief and focused, hands on shoulders, crouched down and face to face. The boys do not move or talk, ideally, and so they must re-focus, catch their breath and think about their actions, whether they think they are doing so or not. And after the allotted time there is conversation, hugs, expressions of sorry, and love.

The time-out has worked very well in our house, and even better when we are consistent and follow our own rules, which can be tough. But when we do, a sense of calm and thoughtfulness pervades our world because of it. Still, the threat of violence can linger right there, not too close, but close none-the-less. Usually this is because I have not utilized the time-out soon enough, allowing some dynamic to play out one beat too long, and now I'm seeing red, and everything happening around me is just noise. It is then especially that I have to remember that it will work eventually. It has to.

And so on another day, it is raining, and we cannot go to the playground, and I just need to get back home. Because I have to get something done for work, but everyone is moving slowly, and complaining about their rain boots, and the lame snacks I brought to pick-up.

And maybe because of all this, Noah is repeating himself.

"Can I have a cookie? Why can't I have a cookie? One cookie, just one. Mommy would give me a cookie," he says, "she totally would."

I could give him a cookie, but then he would be in control. Not that this has to be a power struggle. Why does anyone have to be in control?

"Just one!" he continues.

"Noah, that's a one," I say, still calm.

"You suck," he says.

"Dude, that's a two," I say.

"That's a two," he replies.

Why does his mimicking me put me over the top? And does he know that it does? He must, right? I don't know, I just know that now I am enraged, and that yes, this is a power struggle. I also know that it is still raining, and we are standing on the street, but timeouts can't wait until you get home if you want them to have any kind of impact.

"That's it, bro," I say. "Time-out, here, against that wall. Go stand there for six minutes."

Noah looks at me like I've lost my mind. Then he smiles, but I cannot succumb to that. He's too fucking cute, and I cannot be weak.

"C'mon," he says. "Here? No way."

But I don't budge and I try to breathe and then I turn my back on him. I look at my watch, a minute passes, then two. The rain is fogging my glasses. I do not move. He's quiet. And I am beginning to breathe normally again.

It is then that I feel him wrap his tiny arms around my legs.

"I'm sorry," he says softly.

I smile, I shake my head, I hug him, and we walk home. There has been no violence—the rage has dissipated, and everyone has lived to fight another day.

The Darth Vader Interlude: Dads Who Rock and Those Who Kind of Suck Ass

To be honest, I don't really believe in celebrating fathers as especially rock star or super suck-ass. It's a challenging job and our focus should be on supporting all fathers so they can do the best job possible. Still, that doesn't mean I don't want to know how I rate as a father along the rock/suck-ass father continuum, and so getting a decent handle on the key father metrics is crucial. The following then is my take on the fathers whose awesomeness I can only hope to aspire to and those I clearly blow away.

The Rock Stars:

(1) Nelson Mandela
He was away from home a lot, but otherwise, enough said, right?

(2) Coach Eric Taylor
God damn it, I miss you Coach Taylor. Riggins. Saracen. Smash. Vince. Street. They were all your sons. Clear eyes, full hearts, can't lose, yo.

(3) Atticus Finch
Stare down angry mob? Check. Defend African-American

male in the deep, and still, Jim Crow South? Check. Raise children by yourself? Check. And mate.

(4) Brad Pitt

He's got a lot of children. And Myles says he was very heroic in *World War Z* and should be included for that reason alone. He's also very easy on the eyes.

(5) Cliff Huxtable

It could be the sweaters that I admire. But more likely it is the cool, always calm, demeanor in which he managed all crises, big and small.

(6) Charles Ingalls

You think it's easy out there on the prairie with Scarlet Fever, long winters, and Nelly Olson lurking at every turn. Because it isn't, and yet somehow Charles Ingalls kept smiling. God bless him.

The Suck-Ass:

(1) Darth Vader

Maybe cutting off your son's hand is not such a big deal when it can be so easily replaced, but the rest of it? C'mon, bro.

(2) Ryan O'Neal

Punched-out one son's teeth and hit on his daughter at his girlfriend's funeral. Next.

(3) Marv Marinovich

You want to hire personal trainers from the time your son is born to prepare him for a career in the NFL? Fair enough. But no Twinkies? No. Fuck that.

(4) Don Draper

The dude had it hard as a kid, but fucking your neighbor who is also the mother of your daughter's crush and allowing said daughter to walk in on that? Poor planning is the least of it.

(5) The dad from Cat's in the Cradle

I know when I'm coming home. My boys and I get together. We even throw a ball sometimes. So there's that, which in comparison isn't so bad at all.

(6) Osama bin Laden

Too soon? Just saying.

And the Dad Who's Somewhat Rock Star and Somewhat Suck-Ass All at the Same Time:

Homer Simpson

He loves his children, yet still feels the urge to strangle them. That sounds about right.

No Response

I am at a meeting in a hotel at the end of a service road near O'Hare Airport. The room is small and the table is covered with sweaty pitchers of cold water.

The only reason this is important at all, is that I need to be back in my neighborhood by early afternoon. The boys have a show at school and I promised them that I will be there.

So now I am off and in full sprint, rushing to the train and school, and in the act of doing so, I am ignoring the constant pings on my phone. The texts, Facebook messages, calls, and emails, which are suddenly, and rapidly, coming in.

When I make it to the auditorium, I slump into a chair that Debbie has saved for me catch my breath and finally look at my phone.

There has been a mass shooting at an elementary school in Newtown, Connecticut. Children Noah's age have been killed. The information is still coming in and I ask Debbie if she has read about it. She nods her head yes, lips firmly locked together. I grab her hand, the lights go down, and I try to ignore what I've just read, and watch the boys perform.

"Do you think it's weird that the kids seemingly haven't heard anything about Newtown?" I say to Debbie on the Sunday night following the show.

"It is," she says, "but that just means that we are going to need to say something before someone does at school tomorrow."

"Let's do it in the morning," I say.

We agree that we will focus on what you're supposed to say, that it happened far away from Chicago, and if they are confused about anything, they should ask us. We don't discuss how it will go down, but I wake up first, get them ready for school, and that settles that.

"I need to talk to you guys about something that happened on Friday," I say as we walk to school on Monday morning.

I am holding Noah's hand as Myles zips along beside us. I could have said something at breakfast as they wiped the sleep from their eyes and ate their cereal, but I didn't know if they would go to school after that.

"There was a shooting at a school on Friday," I say, "and Mommy and I want to be sure you hear about it from us and not someone else."

No response.

"The important thing," I continue, "is that it happened far away from here."

"So he can't come here then?" Noah asks.

I wonder how literal I should be with my response.

"No," I say, "the shooter... he hurt himself."

Fuck, that won't be clear. Seven-year olds don't understand euphemisms, and while Myles hasn't reacted yet, he will to this.

"He hurt himself?" Noah asks. "I don't get it."

"He killed himself," Myles says matter-of-factly.

"Oh," Noah says softly.

"And he was probably on drugs or alcohol, right?" Myles asks, already creating a narrative that makes sense to him.

I don't think that is true, but does it matter?

"He might have been," I says. "We don't know, he was probably sick though, and anyway, it was far away from here, and that's important to remember. Also, if you guys hear anything in school today that confuses you, I want you to speak to me or Mommy, okay?"

Nothing, no response, but that is done, for now, and I can breathe again.

I told them it happened far away, just like I tell them that death won't come to them or the people they love for a long time. That's best practice, and it's developmentally appropriate, but that doesn't make it true, and there's the rub.

Myles is only eleven and he has already had a classmate die from cancer, so he knows the idea that death doesn't come for a long time just isn't accurate.

"I don't want to die, ever," Noah says to me one night.

"No one does baby," I say, "but you're a little boy and that isn't going to happen for a long time."

"Can you really say that?" Myles asks leaning over and whispering to me. "Naomi died and she was just a little girl."

I want to tell him to be quiet because this is so not the moment, but he's right, and he will never be able to pretend otherwise.

When the Aurora, Colorado shooting happened, an old friend of mine posted a comment on Facebook asking how gun control advocates could be outraged about that shooting, but not about the daily shootings happening on the streets of Chicago, a city he stressed is known for its leadership on gun control. He also asked how anyone could question the right to carry concealed weapons at a time like this.

I found myself enraged by what I felt was a bullshit comparison—an attack on Chicago, and grandstanding in general.

"I think this post is really inappropriate," I wrote, "your comparisons between the Aurora shooting and shootings in Chicago are specious. Gun control laws here have been gutted, and your timing is disrespectful to the victims."

I didn't mention what I thought about specific gun control laws though, because I was unsure of what works and not confident in my ability to defend them regardless.

"Ben! Fuck you," he wrote back. "My nephew was killed in that movie theater."

Shit.

His response didn't make him right, but I later realized that not unlike Myles and the Newtown shootings, we were both trying to take control of a narrative that upset us and made us feel powerless to protect our children or anyone else's.

I sent him a note to that affect.

"Ben, it's cool," he wrote back. "I forgot about it already. Now go back to writing your stories."

It was clear that he had dismissed me as another liberal, writer, mainstream-media-loving, gun control asshole, but at that point, it was fine. I had said what I wanted to say, and I was happy to re-focus on not having to talk about shootings, gun control, or death.

One month after Newtown, there is an argument one block from the boys' school. It is the culmination of a long running fight between two neighborhood guys that finally comes to an end when one guy draws a gun and the other guy dies.

We can no longer tell the boys that shootings happen far away.

"Why didn't you say something?" Myles says to us accusingly as he stands in the kitchen holding a memo from school that describes the shooting.

"We didn't have a chance," we say.

Which is true, mostly. What we don't say is that we don't want to have that conversation. Shootings in the abstract are bad enough, but this, a shooting in our neighborhood at a corner some of the kids they know have to cross to get to school, how do you explain that?

It's pointless trying to explain to them how a shooting that results from an argument is different than a mass shooting such as Newtown or Aurora, or that mass shootings like Newtown are a small town phenomena, because that doesn't matter to a child. Shot is shot. Dead is dead, and it's either close enough that you can touch it, or it isn't.

Since Aurora and the shootings in Newtown, my neighborhood, and so many other places, it feels impossible not to wish guns would just go away as they have in other places around the world where these things don't seem to happen.

Some of this reaction is selfless. I don't want any more children shot. Some of it is selfish. I really don't want my kids to get shot. And some of it is just denial. I can't even let myself imagine them getting shot, but I know I don't want to discuss it with them anymore and so no guns is a good place to start with that.

The thing is, I know I have felt this way the whole time, and what I wish I could have said to my old high school friend was, "Fuck me? Fuck you. No guns dude, anywhere. How's that? No access, none, period." But I was scared to say that, I didn't want to sound so extreme, and I hate myself now for thinking that way.

After Newtown, that same old friend posted a similar pro-gun screed on his Facebook page, and then another old friend responded, and he said that he had a nephew killed in Newtown. He then went on to say, what I had been unable to say myself.

"Most people may be responsible with their guns, but since so many others are willing to ruin it for the rest of you, too bad, no guns for anyone."

To which I say, amen.

The Boy with the Curious Hair

Winter was coming, and with winter comes the wild-haired beasts from the north, and the other side of the wall: untamed, uninvited, and unpredictable.

Our first baby was due in January, and we were trying to prepare.

You can create a false sense of security though. High walls for example, or if you prefer, baby gates that seem tall enough to protect you from the unknown, when you still have nothing yet to worry about. But can you truly know what to expect? Not really, and not with any confidence certainly.

So you also look for signs to provide you some kind of roadmap for where things might possibly be going, because even a sign that is hard to read or navigate is better than none.

And there was a sign.

Well, there was a sign if you believe in old wives' tales that is. It is said, that a pregnant woman with heartburn is carrying a baby with a full head of hair and Debbie definitely had heartburn.

The thing is, there are lots of old wives' tales when

it comes to pregnancy, weird things that happen with string and needles, ideas about whether the mother is carrying low or high, and so the question is not whether any particular event or experience means anything, but whether you choose to believe that they do.

The trick of course, is that when you want to have a baby, you have to suspend belief at times to get through it. It's safer and easier that way. Think about it. If you consider all of the things that have to go right to create a baby in the first place, there's no guarantee you will get pregnant at all much less that it will go well. Nor is there any guarantee that your baby will be healthy, much less have a full head of hair.

And yet when things start to look good, possible, you will take anything you can get that says it will be okay, that it's going to work, and that helps you makes sense of any of it, at all. Some people might call it denial and I wouldn't disagree.

So, there we were, in the hospital, about to have a baby.

Push. Push. Push. Breathe.

And it was going well.

Push. Push. Push. Breathe.

"Oh my," the doctor says.

Not in panic or anything, just "oh my."

Push. Push. Push. Breathe.

"What, what," we say. "What is it?"

"It's the hair," she says. "This baby has so much hair. It's all I can see."

Push. Push. Push. Breathe.

We could not see it though, not at first anyway. But soon it came forth, a tangled, dark mass of tendrils, splaying out with each push.

For some time after that the hair was all we had to go on.

Push. Hair. Push. Hair. Push. Hair. Breathe. No hair. Push. Hair. Push.

But then, wait, a head, a malformed head, no, that's wrong, it's not malformed, not exactly, just face down, and covered, covered with hair. It is mesmerizing. We don't know what to do, or say, but then the baby rolls over, and the baby looks up at us.

It is beautiful, and it is a boy, our boy, Myles, the first one, the older one, always, and forever.

He is whisked away. They spray his eyes until they are clear of junk and scrub his little body until it's pink. They wash his hair and remove the muck. They swaddle him and bring him back to us. His hair is lighter now and spiky, shooting off in all directions. It's wonderful and we cannot get enough of it.

"It will fall out," the nurses tell us.

"Yeah," they say, "my kid had hair like that, maybe not quite like that, that's unbelievable, but he had a lot of it, and it fell out. It grew back though, don't worry. It was lovely, like goose down, you'll see."

So we wait, but the hair doesn't go away. It just keeps growing. Soon it's long and flowing, and then it gets lighter still, like honey. Little curls appear and Myles becomes our Samson, not to mention our Luke Skywalker, Captain Kirk, Ned Stark, Bilbo, Aragorn, Silver Surfer, Harry Potter, John Carter, Bill Murray, and Patrick Ewing.

He looks like no other baby you have ever seen. Of course, he is no other baby. He's ours.

People stop us on the street so they can touch his hair. It begins to crawl out from underneath his knit caps like the grungy alternative rockers on MTV. Back when MTV showed videos anyway.

Regardless, we love him and we love the hair.

Before long though the people change, they turn on us, and they want to know when we plan to cut his hair.

"It's too long now," they say.

"You can barely see his face."

"It's not so cute anymore."

But it is to us, and we're so very attached to it. It's his calling card. It's what makes him Myles, and we're cool with that, until we're not. The hair once so beautiful becomes flat and tangled. Cowlicks start to appear, as do swirls of hair on the back of his head that look like little birds' nests. It's messy and his face is getting lost.

Debbie and I talk about getting it cut.

"There's a kid's place," Debbie says. "They have race-cars for children to sit in. It's fun and cute and it's time."

She's right of course, and I know this, but even though I've been talking about it, I realize I am still so very resistant to actually doing it.

"What if he cries when we put him in the seat?"

He's just starting to do such things.

"And we will have to watch the time. We don't want to throw-him off his nap schedule, do we? Or conversely, put him through such a thing when he's tired, right?"

These are excuses though, diversions, and yes, again, denial. I don't want that hair cut. I don't want Myles to be something else. He is our Samson, and what is going to happen when he no longer has his cowlicky, yet still awesome, flowing hair?

Will he still be able to do battle with the White Walkers when they appear at the Wall, protecting not just those he loves, but the Seven Kingdoms in all of there wide-ranging awesomeness? Will he even be able to scale the Wall with his wilding lover in the first place? Or any wall for that matter? What if he we rob him of his strength before he even gets started? Who knows what great and heroic things he may yet have done, until we succumbed to peer pressure and cut his hair.

I see Myles on a spaceship, hurtling through time and space, his long, beautiful hair flowing out of his space helmet like a rock star, his mission to save the earth from itself, the rising oceans, the flooding, the harsh winters, the lack of food, and intense heat, where dogs and cats now live together, unless he can fight his way across the galaxy, doing battle not only with the White Walkers, but Magneto, the Syrens, Darth Vader, Walter White, The Terminator, President Coriolanus Snow, Loki, Dick Cheney, The Baseball Furies, Voldemort, the Golem, and Gollum, as he finds his fellow citizens a new world to call home, and because he is so full of benevolence and fairness, he becomes its first leader, and the face on the new dollar bill for time immemorial.

And yet, while that all seems so very possible, there we are one morning in the hair salon just shy of his first birthday. There are chairs there shaped like racecars as Debbie said, and spaceships as well, which is nice. Each chair faces its own television on which children's videos are constantly playing—*Elmo* and *Rolie Polie Olie*, *The Wiggles*, and *The Teletubbies*. There is also a toy room in the back. It has faux rock walls. It is meant to look like a cave and little kids run in and out of it, endlessly screaming and fighting.

Myles and I play in there until it is his turn and then they place him in his little car. He's decked-out in a blue crew neck sweater and khakis and he looks like such a big boy. He is all smiles, even as the kid in the rocket ship next to him starts to cry.

I wonder if this will set Myles off as well, but he's cool. The hairdresser places little purple barrettes in his hair. He starts chewing on her spray bottle. The kid keeps crying, but not Myles, he does not budge, or fuss.

And so she starts.

Snip. Snip. Snip.

She adjusts his head. He's fine. She checks for evenness. No problem.

Snip. Snip. Snip.

She moves the barrettes. Still fine. She sprays a little more water. He smiles.

Snip. Snip. Snip.

Myles is chilling, his hair falling away curl by curl, and floating to the ground like the fall leaves do on a windy day. As the hair falls away Myles' face emerges.

Snip. Snip. Snip.

It's no longer such a baby face. Not so round or plump any more. He has a distinct little chin. There are angles and points. You can see his eyes more clearly, the slight Asiatic influence from my father's side of the family more obvious.

As I continue to watch tears begin to well up in my eyes.

Snip. Snip. Snip.

My throat begins to tighten.

Snip. Snip. Snip.

My chest starts to hurt a little as well and I turn away for a moment. Our baby is disappearing before our eyes.

I look back at Myles as the hairdresser finishes the job. He looks at me, he smiles, and he lifts his arms up above his head so that I can pick him up. And I do, gladly, and sadly. I squeeze him to me as the tears flow down my cheeks. I get a waft of his intoxicating Myles smell and nuzzle his wonderful little neck. Then I pull away and I look at Myles' no longer baby face. As I get lost amongst the sharp angles, I am reminded that things didn't turn out well for Ned Stark. I also begin to see a different narrative for him, and while this narrative may be fraught with denial as well, that doesn't mean it can't be real, or true. It's just that we don't know anything about him yet, and we won't, until we do, because before that, it's all signs and guesswork and hope.

In this narrative, Myles is a good man, he doesn't do battle with the White Walkers or the Golem, any more than he finds himself hurtling through space. Instead, he is kind and caring. He volunteers his time, and fights for social justice. He hates inequality and oppression of all kinds. He is a good friend and brother, a community leader, a loving husband and father. He grows old as people do, he goes to work, he pays his bills, and while sometimes great things happen for him, other times he feels profound disappointments and loss. He keeps moving forward though, he takes care of those around him, he is curious, and he leads a long, full life.

Having great hair and slaying dragons are pretty cool things, but living well can be heroic too, and how can any parent ask for more than that?

My Vasectomy

There I was one day in my urologist's office talking about my kidney stones, which I had learned were the result of my poor hydration and the fact that I was consuming too much spinach.

Really.

The conversation went like this:

"The problem is spinach. That and you don't drink enough water," my doctor said.

"Spinach, though, really?" I asked.

"Well, and too much black tea. And cranberries," he said.

"I'm sorry, so it's spinach, tea, and cranberries? Why did I give up drugs, again?" I asked.

He didn't respond to that, so I decided to switch gears and I asked him about vasectomies instead. He immediately got into the potential side effects.

"One side effect is that you can suffer from painful orgasms," my doctor said.

"Every time?" I said.

"Every time," he said.

"Just to clarify," I said. "This entire exchange revolves

around my achieving orgasm in an ongoing fashion regardless, though, correct?"

"It does," he said.

"Then we're probably fine," I said.

"I can perform it right here in my office," the doctor said.

"Really, right here?" I said.

"Totally," he said. "It's not even surgery. It's just a procedure."

"Yeah? How does that affect your use of anesthesia?" I asked. I watch *Grey's Anatomy* and I'm kind of an expert on medical things.

"There's no anesthesia," he said. "We just numb the area."

I wondered how that's possible. Not the numbing part, because I'd done that before, right there in his sterile, freezing office before, my dick in a clamp, fastened in place so he could look at my kidneys, his smoking hot young resident standing nearby as my penis shrank, and I morphed into George Costanza.

"You don't understand! There is shrinkage!" I had yelled to little affect.

Of course, if this had been *Grey's*, she would have given me a hug and a happy ending, albeit for purely medical reasons. But sadly, this was not *Grey's*, and we are no longer talking about kidney stones. It's a vasectomy: there will be a tug, a snip, and then no more semen, no more children, no nothing, just like that. And you can just do that in an office without anesthesia. Shouldn't it be more monumental? I will be relinquishing my ability to reproduce. Shouldn't there at least be mid-tempo Gregorian chants, or balloons, because, ultimately, if it's just an out-patient procedure, it really doesn't mean much, does it?

I suppose it shouldn't bother me. It's not like I want more children.

Well, maybe that's not entirely accurate. It is nearly impossible to see the little girls my boys play with and not wonder what it would be like to raise one, and then watch her play in the NCAA women's basketball Final Four for Princeton, become a Rhodes Scholar, and eventually serve as Senator, possibly from New Jersey, though Illinois would be fine, too.

But to have another screaming baby in the house, maybe one with colic, potential speech problems, holes in their spines, SIDS, teasing, fear of school shootings, porch parties, predators, busy streets, bath salts, and on, and on? No thanks.

I also don't plan to be one of those guys who willingly delays his vasectomy for the moment when he's older and finds himself married to a brunette, former Olympic volleyball player turned professional dancer turned documentary filmmaker somewhere loosely between the ages of twenty-five to thirty-five who wants a child. Not that I have thought much about this. But that doesn't mean it isn't possible, the re-married part anyway, and the younger woman. Not that I want to be re-married either, and not that I have any plans to that affect, it's just that with life decisions come possibilities, scenarios, and questions of what might be.

You decide to have children and someone says you need a will. Why is this? You didn't before. But you do now, and now you have to answer questions you hadn't previously considered. How should your estate be divided? Who should divide it? And where should your children go to live if, in fact, you find yourself on a plane flying from Australia to Los Angeles that mysteriously crashes, and by some chance of fate, you are not one of the Oceanic Six?

What then? Had I ever thought about death before that? I had not. Do I think about it now? All the time, which leads to another matter I never thought much about, life insurance, why it actually exists, and for that matter, the meaning of the word "insurance."

It's there in case something happens. I had never thought about the possibility that something might happen to me, which isn't to say that I thought I was immortal either. It's just that I never thought about it at all. And why would I?

"I think I want a full million dollars if you die," Debbie says when we are discussing life insurance. "I think it's worth paying for."

"Sure," I say wondering where this is going. I'm married and so I know it's going somewhere.

"It's just that, I may end up alone," she says, "and

so the money will be really nice. But you, you won't be alone, so you don't need as much insurance. Why waste the money, right?"

So that's where this is going. This had never crossed my mind before. Well, that's not exactly true. I have calculated the age difference between myself and Selena Gomez many times, though only after she and Justin Bieber had clearly called it quits. They got into that thing in a nightclub. It was like a dance-off or something, right? But had I really considered being with someone else? Not until now.

"I think you're right," I say, "I may not be alone, and it pains me to say this, but if by some chance I'm not, and if by some equally unlikely chance Selena Gomez is still single, she will have needs I sadly cannot meet, and expensive tastes, and so that full million is going to be a big help. You understand that, right?"

All of which is to say, that anything is possible, and so why not plan accordingly?

So I ask my doctor, "How do you measure the success rate of a vasectomy without testing it the old fashioned way?"

"You need to orgasm one hundred times," my doctor says, "and then you come in and we test the fluid to confirm there is no semen present."

"Whoa, one-hundred times," I'm incredulous. It might have taken a whole week to reach that in high school, but now, that could be years. "Can you write my wife a note requiring her assistance with that?"

"I can suggest it," he says, "but it probably won't help much."

Which may have been true, but I suppose it's also time for full disclosure: I never actually had a vasectomy.

Why didn't I have one?

It could be the orgasms. The likelihood of painful orgasms is low, but is it worth the risk?

I can vividly recall the first orgasm I had after my bladder was scoped and my urologist was briefly concerned I might actually have a tumor and not a hidden kidney stone.

Luckily I was by myself, in a hotel room in New Mexico, and thinking about Georgia O'Keefe, because while the dread and anticipation was excruciating enough, the experience itself was like an explosion of broken glass. It was the best broken glass ever, mind you, even better than Bag O'Glass, but broken glass is still broken glass. Did I want that every time I orgasmed without fail?

Debbie says she does not want that for me. She has insisted it's not worth the risk. Which is fine, I suppose, but isn't it my turn to carry the birth control load? She's been carrying it for much of this relationship, so why not me, and why not now?

Or more accurately, why haven't I pushed it more?

I remember when I was a child and my father came home one day from the doctor's office and collapsed onto the couch with an ice pack. It was light blue and kicked around the house for years, the rubber coating slowly flaking off, and the melted ice sure to drip all over everything.

Anyway, my father told me he had hurt his knee, though that didn't explain why he was icing his balls or looked so beaten-down, a faded version of his normal self. He was a tough guy, and I wanted to be like him: tough, fearless, invincible, settling things with my fists. And yet to see him like that, compromised, and then to later realize why—perhaps this has the most to do with my inaction?

There is part of me that wonders what you give up when you give this up. Do you end-up like Samson. Because I'm not ready to feel less powerful. I have too much misplaced pride, and I am too caught up in what I think it means to be a man, and to be like my dad, even if he had a vasectomy himself.

Any or all of this is possible, of course, though there's another possibility as well.

Despite my protestations, I still may want to be a father again. The fact is, there's too much joy involved in it, and yes, too much pride, not to want to. It's a different kind of pride, but it is also a better pride, the pride you have watching your children grow up and become something amazing. Because that's what they do, most of them anyway, and most of the time.

Acknowledgments

There is no *Lost In Space* without the Myles and Noah, so let's start right there with their beautiful mugs. There is also no Myles and Noah without the Debbie, or a me without my mom and dad, so that's cheesy, but let's do that too. Cool? Awesome. Thank you.

There is also the Victor David Giron and his Maker's Mark infused encouragement, as well as, the awesomely wide-ranging and electric Curbside crew, Jacob, Emma, Naomi, Catherine, Leonard, Richard, Mikaela, and on and on.

Appreciations to the *NAILED*, *The Good Men Project*, *Gigantic Sequins*, *The Rumpus*, *Abroad View*, *Midnight Mind*, *Monkey Bicycle*, *Chicago Parent*, and *The Weeklings*, where a number of these pieces were previously published in some form somewhat approximating the form they're in now.

Much thank to my blurbers, Jennifer Banash, Paula Bomer, Jillian Lauren, Joshua Mohr, and Patrick Wensink, they all rock, and are all ridiculously attractive. Which is nice.

Awe for the Steve Lafler and Alban Fischer for their artistry and mad design skills.

Big props to the Leah Tallon who is blessed with a light touch, grand insights, and a load of greatness.

And endless love to *Mad Men*, Patrick Ewing, Chicago, Selena Gomez, *Game of Thrones*, *The Walking Dead*, Lady Gaga, *The Lion King*, the X-Men, *Orange Is The New Black*, Lindsay Lohan, Chuck Klosterman, the David, Natalie Portman, *LOST*, *Ghost Dog: Way of the Samurai*, Vanilla Ice, Yoda, *Caddyshack*, and David Sedaris, inspirations all, yo.

Ben Tanzer is the author of *My Father's House*, *You Can Make Him Like You*, *So Different Now*, and *Orphans*, among others. Ben serves as Director of Publicity and Content Strategy at Curbside Splendor Publishing and can be found online at This Blog Will Change Your Life, the center of his growing lifestyle empire. He lives in Chicago with his wife and two sons.

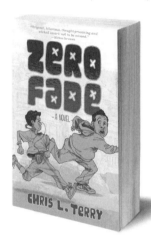
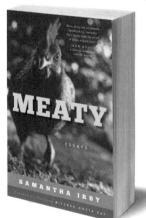